CW00545013

Malcolm Root's
TRANSPORT PAINTINGS

Malcolm Root's
TRANSPORT PAINTINGS

TEXT BY
TOM TYLER

HALSGROVE

First published in 2002 by Halsgrove
Images © 2002 Malcolm Root
Text © 2002 Tom Tyler

All rights reserved. No part of this publication may be reproduced,
stored in a retrieval system, or transmitted in any form or by any means
without the prior permission of the copyright holder.

British Library Cataloguing-in-Publication Data
A CIP record for this title is available from the British Library

ISBN 1 84114 221 2

HALSGROVE
Halsgrove House
Lower Moor Way
Tiverton, Devon EX16 6SS
T: 01884 243242
F: 01884 243325
www.halsgrove.com

Printed and bound in Italy by Centro Grafico Ambrosiano

Foreword
by Lord Montagu of Beaulieu

The period since the early 1960s has seen an amazing growth in the movement to preserve every aspect of our country's transport heritage, whether it be road vehicles, railways, aircraft or ships. Not only are thousands of vehicles now preserved, some in museums, many more by private owners, but they are supported by a network of owners clubs, and a wealth of literature.

Malcolm Root's paintings not only portray the vehicles of the past era with scrupulous accuracy, but they also take us back to the period in question through excellent attention to detail, and painstaking research. Costume, advertisements, road signs, buildings, luggage, even the child's pram, all evoke memories and add to the realism of the scene.

At Beaulieu we have a living museum, where we preserve not only the vehicles of past days, but the accessories, such as the garage, which go with them. We also display vehicles such as 'Chitty Chitty Bang Bang' for limited periods, and mount exhibitions, as in 2001 when 'Motoring through Childhood' was the theme. We seek to recreate the whole motoring scene from the past, and in this respect there is a harmony between the National Motor Museum here at Beaulieu, and Malcolm Root's painting, in which he achieves the same goal. In this book he portrays a B-type bus crossing Westminster Bridge, while we run such a bus taking our visitors round the museum grounds every day. I am also proud of the fact that in 1957, as a result of an inaugural rally of historic commercial vehicles held here at Beaulieu, the Historic Commercial Society was founded, and I have been its president for many years.

Those who are of an older generation will find this book, or a visit to Beaulieu, to be a nostalgic trip into a much loved past, and there can be no harm in that in an age where speed seems to be the only thing that matters. This book will touch the chord of memory for so many people, and bring much enjoyment as it does so.

Montage of Beaulieu

Lord Montagu of Beaulieu
August 2002

Norfolk Charabanc
Painted 2000

It certainly looks like a race, and no doubt the train driver has eased his regulator a little further open! The charabanc, based in North Lincolnshire is 1919 vintage, but the Darracq behind, manfully trying to keep up, is much earlier. The Beyer Peacock 4-4-0 of the M & GNR (Midland & Great Northern Railway) is the oldest of the three, having been built in the late 1880s. The road surface leaves much to be desired, but there are some excellent horse droppings to be gathered for someone's roses, and the whole scene conjures up an atmosphere of noise, dust, smoke and speed!

Introduction

For some people this book may seem to be no more than a selection of paintings by a gifted and versatile artist. I would suggest it is much more than that. It is in fact a chronicle of the transport of our own times, and transport has made a huge contribution to the development and everyday life of our nation.

Here you have the simple one-horsepower cart contrasted with the coal lorry, the steam wagon with the mighty eight-wheel lorry. You have the development of farming, from threshing machine to combine harvester. You have the Dragon Rapide biplane giving help to vehicles of twenty years later, and the pre-war Dakota contrasted with the Comet jet airliner. The small steamer that serves the outer Scottish islands is compared to the mightiest of the Cunard liners, and the modern Stena Discovery moves past a sailing barge almost a century old. Cars from the turn of the twentieth century rub shoulders with the Docklands Light Railway from the turn of the twenty-first century. Malcolm Root has set all these carefully portrayed means of transport in their true context, with meticulous attention to detail not only of the vehicles, but buildings, rural and urban scenes, and costume.

As I came to write the text for this book, the paintings rekindled for me a strong affection for the transport of past decades, especially the period of the 1940s and 50s when I was growing up, and eventually owned my first car. I was constantly reminded what fun motoring was, and at times quite an adventure as well. It was a time when we did pick up hitchhikers, almost as a duty, without any thought of possible consequences; when we would stop to help someone in trouble, assisting in the changing of a wheel, or the drying out of a distributor cap. A roadside picnic was part of the day's enjoyment, not spoilt by noise and fumes; a St Christopher badge on the dashboard acknowledged the need for a bit of Divine providence if we were going to make our home port in safety!

I have to admit, also, that occasionally I was led to feel that not everything has improved on the Queen's highway over the years, and the reader may find a suspicion of this attitude at times! However, I must say that to write the text for these paintings has been a great privilege and joy, and it has taken me to new places, and to meet new people, all of whom have been helpful and encouraging. I should especially like to acknowledge my gratitude to Gordon Sly for farming information, and to Brian Dyers and Bob Mellor and staff at the Ipswich Transport Museum; to Wilfrid Tyler for help over motorcycles, and to the staff at the AA for much information. I should also like to record my thanks to my daughter Clare for invaluable help with a new-fangled computer thing that seems to have many characteristics which my old typewriter did not possess!

I could never have written the text for this book without the boundless help and wide knowledge of Malcolm Root himself. The inspiration is mainly his, while the mistakes, feeble jokes and stick-in-the-mud attitude are definitely all my own!

Tom Tyler

Artist's Introduction

With a brand new white A3 (or the imperial equivalent) sheet of paper placed in front of me, the problem was, 'Now, what to draw?' This was the problem for a seven-year-old at 'little school' in the late 1950s, and the reward for redoing his simple sums correctly. Armed with some wax crayons, some barely an inch long, some (the most sought after) brand new, I was ready to make a start. This is where the young mind would start to remember the things that had made an impression on him, whether it was a bus journey to the nearest big town, or perhaps a train journey to the seaside.

Nowadays, with modern transport, the object would seem to be to get to your destination as soon as possible, but in those days the journey was (to me anyway) as important as the day out. It is no surprise then that the first marks made on the paper would represent some sort of transport. The seeds were sown.

When eventually our family owned a car and a long journey was undertaken, sandwich stops would invariably be taken beside a railway line or at some distance from an airfield runway where we would be lucky to see any movement at all in the time allowed. I remember one occasion, at Boscombe Down, the approach of an AA patrolman on his motorcycle to enquire whether we would like to become members of the Association. He must have done his job well for my father joined there and then. Could this have been in my mind when I painted the picture 'What seems to be the trouble?'

Other influences imposed themselves as time passed. It was a revolutionary era for car design. Who could forget the introduction of the Mini or the 'all new' Ford Anglia? These were represented in model form with the now famous and very collectable Dinkys and Corgis, and the not-so-famous Spot On models. A visit to the dentist or hospital would sometimes – if I was lucky – be rewarded with a Corgi model, and this would be the fuel for further picture matter. Through paintings I could reconstruct scenes that held many memories for me, something that has stayed with me to this day. This I hope is reflected in some way in the pages of this book.

Throughout the history of painting, artists have in the main recorded their present. This was once the only way to do so but the advent of photography provided another method. It could be argued that this has released some artists to indulge themselves in nostalgia. I make no apology for falling into this category for there is something very rewarding about the gathering of information and memories to produce an historic painting unrecorded by photograph. There is today a competitor in 'digital' photography, with technology and techniques which are spreading at an ever increasing rate. Despite this, I think that a painting has that little bit extra. But then I would, wouldn't I?

The Paintings

Colchester Tram
Painted 2001

The Colchester Tramway opened in the year 1904, with a fleet of 16 trams, to provide modern transport through a town which dated back to Roman times. The trams, supplied by Dick Kerr & Company, had bodies made by the British Electric Wagon & Carriage Co. Ltd at Preston, mounted on Brill 21E trucks. These had two 35hp motors. In 1906 two further trams were added to the fleet, identical to the others except that they had direct instead of reverse staircases. For the inaugural run on 28 July 1904 the Lady Mayoress, Mrs E.H. Barritt drove tram no. 13 to Lexden. The fleet was decommissioned in 1928, and the trams sold to Mr Moss, a builder, for use as site huts. Over the years some were burnt, but no. 10 is still partly in existence though well hidden!

In the picture, tram no. 10 is seen ascending Lexden Hill in the afternoon, on its way to the tram terminus. In Colchester, the trams operated out of a depot in Magdalen Street in the centre of town, where they were also cleaned and maintained. Trams were quiet, economical on fuel, and pollution free. The only disadvantage was the overhead wires and the rails – the latter could produce a problem like that so vividly depicted in the film *Genevieve*, when the veteran car's wheels stuck in the tram rails and it was guided the wrong way like a railway wagon! The trams were a significant feature of the town scene, both before and after the First World War, until they were replaced with motor buses.

The need to find a road used by trams and one that has changed little in one hundred years is an obvious one. This task was not too difficult in a town I know well. Sunlight and shadows are important ingredients in a picture to give depth and substance. When I arrived at the spot one Saturday afternoon to make colour notes and take some photographs the sun was in a position that made the buildings look 'flat'. Another hour or two and the sun would move round to cast the shadows as seen in the painting. Fortunately, and very conveniently, a pub was at hand to while away the time – the progress of the sun being monitored relative to the level in my glass. Such is the life of an artist!

Sherwood's Atkinson
Painted 2000

This is a familiar scene to be found in the backstreets of many a town. The old factory building, probably dating back to Victorian times, has outlived its usefulness, and the time has come for demolition to allow the building of a more modern building on the increasingly valuable site. However, many of the old materials which are worth saving are being loaded by hand on to the Atkinson lorry supplied by Sherwood's, haulage contractors from Hull. Those materials past recycling are being burnt. Meanwhile, the driver and the foreman in charge of demolition discuss details of the work.

Sherwood's obviously went for quality, as the Atkinson eight-wheel lorry shown in the picture was a cut above the Fords, Bedfords and Austins of the day. Atkinson began in business back in 1907, when they offered a service repairing steam wagons. The first Atkinson steam wagon was produced in 1916, but sadly the company, like many others, floundered financially during the depression. Atkinson was reconstructed as Atkinson Lorries Ltd in 1933, and began producing four- and six-wheel lorries. The eight-wheel lorry shown was introduced in 1937. Atkinson lorries were solidly built, with the emphasis on strength and reliability. Recently one that had stood forgotten in a field for twenty or more years was given some oil and a new battery, and started up at once, ready for work! The vehicles were powered by Gardiner diesel engines, which would not have been particularly easy to start using the prominent starting handle.

Although the vehicle is usually the main focus of pictures within this book, the location or background is of equal importance and often forms the story behind the painting. A demolition site would not be everyone's idea of a picture, but when seen on a visit to Hull the colour and 'hanging rooms' had an instant appeal. Although a modern scene it was reminiscent of the bomb sites that were all too common in our cities. The Atkinson eight-wheeler seemed an appropriate choice, and the name Sherwoods was added as a thank-you to our friends Bob and Jean Sherwood (no connection to the haulage firm), who so kindly opened their home to us.

The Lotus and the Windmill
Painted 1999

Lotus Engineering Co. Ltd was the company set up in February 1953 by Colin Chapman, a brilliant engineer and designer who by that date had already produced a number of special cars for racing and trials. The company began by producing kit cars, to which a customer could add a choice of components. The Lotus Elan launched in October 1962 could be purchased either as a complete car, for £1500, or in kit form for £1095. The Lotus Elan shown in the picture is a Plus 2S 130, introduced in 1971, and the last of the line, the cars being discontinued in 1973. In all about 3000 of these models were built. The engine was the same as that fitted to the Lotus Sprint and developed 126bhp at 5500rpm. Weber carburettors were fitted to these models, replacing the earlier Stromberg design, and in October 1972 a five-speed gearbox was offered as an optional extra.

Saxtead Windmill is located at Saxtead Green, a few miles north-west of Framlingham in Suffolk. The beautifully restored mill is a postmill, designed so that the whole upper body rotates, moved by a small windmill so that the sails are always head to wind. The mill is owned by English Heritage and is typical of many East Anglian windmills of the past, which did much varied work in a flat and windy landscape. Saxtead Windmill was commercially milling wheat corn right up to the outbreak of the First World War.

A Night on the Town

Painted 1994

You can almost taste the candy floss in this evocative picture of Southend promenade at night! Seven Daimler CWA6 buses were bought by Southend Corporation in 1955 from Eastern National. These buses had been new in 1943–45, and consequently the 56-seat bodies had been built to utility war standards. When more modern buses were acquired in 1956, five of the old Daimlers were taken into the works and converted to become open-top buses. Seafront services were then operated with these buses. Once a year the buses had their day out, running a day excursion to the Derby at Epsom. This must have been a pretty stiff endurance test for the top-deck passengers, not only if it rained, but because it involved many miles sitting on wooden slatted seats! Originally, the buses had very low fronts, but later a windscreen was fitted to give the top deck a little more protection.

Bus no. 244 was saved from the breakers initially by the Beamish Museum in County Durham where the author had a ride on the top deck, but it has since returned to its old home, Southend, and is cared for by the Castle Point Transport Museum Society. The five buses remained in service until 1970, but even in those modern times, while it was in order for the buses to parade topless, lady passengers were firmly discouraged from doing so!

In front of the Pier Casino can be seen a Standard Eight, which was the 803cc model introduced in 1953. It was a neat little saloon which the makers claimed would do 45mpg at 45mph – good figures for those days.

Royal Mail Van
Painted 1993

A little snow would never stop the postman doing his rounds, but as you can see it does provide wonderful ammunition for a snowball fight on the way to school. This scene is the flatter countryside of East Anglia. In the author's native Devon the postman, and others, had to put on wheel chains to cope with the many and steep hills when it snowed. Here the postman has already done his first round delivering letters, and is emptying the pillar boxes – in this case a beautiful one set in a brick-arched pillar, at the time that the children are going into school. The postman was always a good friend to the whole community, and had time to assist a young lady to post her letter. In the author's home village a large boulder about 18-inches high was placed below the pillar box so that children could climb up to post letters more easily.

Morris supplied all the vans for the Post Office. The van in the picture is a Y-model Morris van, first introduced in 1939 when the Post Office took delivery of two vehicles. By 1945 there were 2000 in service, and most of these were still in use in 1960, a good testimony to their design and reliability. Rated as a 10cwt van, the Y-model was powered by a four-cylinder sidevalve engine rated at 1547cc. Drive was through a three-speed gearbox. The vans were not economical on fuel, but then few vehicles would be with the constant stopping and starting. In those days of few vehicles, it looks as though the mail van may have been the only vehicle up and down the road before school time. In those days all the children walked to school, some from several miles away, snow or no snow!

*The flexibility offered by painting means that summer scenes can be turned into winter and vice versa.
Such is the case with this picture of the Royal Mail van. Our friendly (and efficient, I might add) postman was
able to suggest this distinctive postbox in a nearby village, where he posed with his modern van. The summer
was turned to winter, the modern van to a Morris Y-model van, and schoolchildren added to complete the scene.
A way of preventing global warming with the stroke of a brush!*

Northern Star
Painted 2001

This beautiful painting shows a three-quarter view of the liner with the sun rising out of the sea behind her. *Northern Star* was built by Vickers Armstrong and launched by Queen Elizabeth the Queen Mother on 27 June 1961. She made her maiden voyage for the Shaw Savill Line in July 1962, and she was put on the route from Southampton to Australia and New Zealand via either Capetown and the eastern route, or else westward via Panama. She was built as a companion vessel to the *Southern Cross* but even on her maiden voyage she experienced trouble with her Parson's high-pressure turbines. Though she reached Sydney, the turbines failed again on departure from Tahiti, and by the time the ship arrived back in Southampton she was nine days late on her schedule.

In 1970 the *Southern Cross* was withdrawn from service, and in 1974 Shaw Savill withdrew the *Northern Star*, following a final cruise beginning on 1 November. The ship had a working life of only twelve years, and should have had many more years of service to come. However, she was the victim of the vast increase in easier and cheaper air traffic during the late 1960s and 70s. Having had the experience of a sea voyage from Southampton to Sydney, taking about

five weeks, it must be stated that there was a lot to be said for a rapid journey, relatively speaking, and much more time to spend exploring the countries when one reached them.

Pickfords' Scammell

Painted 1996

Pickfords, heavy-haulage specialists since the late 1920s, had a great reputation for moving anything, anywhere, and whatever the weather, so it is appropriate that we have a spectacular thunderstorm raging here. Under the watchful eye of a policeman, and the driver's mate, a huge pressure vessel is being delivered to Woolwich Docks. Such boilers might have to travel many miles on much narrower roads than today's, causing major traffic congestion. Drivers also had to be very skilled to handle such huge loads.

Scammell Lorries Ltd was founded in 1922 after an old-established firm of coachbuilders, G. Scammell and Nephew Ltd had experimented with a prototype four-wheel tractor and two-wheel semi-trailer. In the 1920s and 30s Scammell built ever larger and more powerful four- and six-wheel tractors, powered mainly by Gardiner diesel engines, and capable of hauling enormous loads on purpose-built trailers like the forty-eight-wheel example shown. Also caught up in the event are three cars. The Ford Prefect on the right is the 1939 Model 93A, rated at 10hp. On the left is an SS Jaguar 1.5-litre sidevalve 4, and behind it may be lurking a Riley 12 Model 29S saloon.

An unusual feature of this area was the triple tramlines, with power supplied to the vehicles via a centre rail, while the wheels ran on the two outside rails which also conducted power. The centre rail consisted of a conduit open at the top, with a sunken centre rail, and the tram had a trailing shoe that made contact to pick up power. Only a very persistently kamikaze pedestrian would have managed self-electrocution, but one feels water and debris must have been a problem at times.

Liverpool Street Taxi
Painted 2000

In London, during the great days of the railways, the flagship termini were Paddington, Euston, King's Cross and Victoria. Liverpool Street, the second station for the LNER (London and North Eastern Railway), was situated towards the East End of the city, and operated an intense suburban service. Although longer-distance trains went to Colchester, Ipswich and Norwich, the London terminus always seemed rather bleak, down-to-earth and functional. Since those days Liverpool Street has had a considerable facelift, and is much brighter and more welcoming.

The London taxi into which two grateful travellers are putting their luggage is the Austin FX3, first introduced in June 1948. The scene must be soon after the new taxi came into service, as the teak coaches in the background still bear the LNER lettering – something which was not changed after nationalisation, for several years in certain cases. The Austin FX3 was designed so that the driver was completely enclosed, but the front luggage area had no door, and luggage could be secured with straps if necessary. The engine on this new model was based on the Austin 16hp-saloon, and was claimed to do 17–18mpg in urban conditions. A novel feature was the introduction of fluid jacks on all four wheels, powered by a hydraulic pump on the engine. Front or rear wheels could be jacked up independently, or all four wheels together. It could have provided a novel way of thwarting car thieves! The cost of this taxi, to which was added double purchase tax, led to a decrease in the number on the streets of London by 1953.

Meccano Van
Painted 1996

In this picture Malcolm Root has painted a portrait of an actual Bedford 5-ton van, BEK 343, which was first registered in Wigan, Lancashire, and which would have operated from the famous Meccano factory in Binns Road, Liverpool. This large van, one of the range of 'Big Bedfords', was introduced in the 1950s. Built at the Vauxhall plant at Luton, it was specially equipped with a Pallet-Jekta telescopic floor for loading goods on pallets.

By the 1950s the production of Meccano Dinky Toys was at its peak. Dinky Toys were quite heavy, being made from die-cast metal, and also quite bulky as they were by this time packaged in individual boxes. Thus a roomy van, and careful handling were essential.

Frank Hornby, who was born in 1863, longed to be an inventor from a early age. It was not until 1901 that he took out a patent for the constructional toy, Meccano, and it was nearly twenty years later, in 1920, that the well-known trains that bear his name followed. In 1932 'Modelled Miniatures' first appeared in a trade catalogue – metal models of people, animals and a bus and railcar. These were renamed Dinky Toys in 1934, and were an instant success.

During the war, production ceased, and in the years immediately afterwards Dinky Toys were very hard to find, especially for us country dwellers. By the time one got to the shop the small ration had long since gone. The author's mother solved the problem by bartering fresh eggs for the reserving of a few of the precious Dinkys until someone could arrive to collect them!

The other vehicles in the picture are a two-door Morris Minor saloon, with a 948cc engine, introduced in 1954. Behind the Bedford van can be seen a Morris Y-model van, as shown on page 11.

The attraction of gadgets to young boys is a strong one, and a friend of mine was no exception. On this occasion the gadget was a powerful magnet. As he was passing the toyshop shown in the painting, the row of matchbox cars standing on their boxes was too great a temptation to resist. The magnet was placed against the glass window and some of the cars moved from their boxes. This must have puzzled shop staff the following morning!

Westminster Bridge

Painted 1998

This painting of one of the best-known views in the world is the setting for a trio of the London General Omnibus Co. B-type buses, carefully posed so that both front and rear views of the vehicles can be seen. This bus was the epitome of utility, with a sturdy chassis, four solid wheels, a reliable and simple engine, and a carrying compartment for perhaps 36 passengers, seated on hard wooden seats. Yet this omnibus was to be the forerunner of thousands of red double-decker buses which have become an essential feature of London life over the past ninety years. They may indeed get bigger, faster and more comfortable, but the B-type was the first of the line.

The B-type was also the world's first mass-produced passenger vehicle, and this became of great importance upon the outbreak of the First World War in August 1914. Hundreds of the buses were shipped over to France to provide transport for the troops, and they did sterling work despite the fact that the top deck must have been an even more uncomfortable place than usual with quantities of shrapnel flying around!

The tramlines, and the Panhard London taxi of 1910, which provided more comfortable travel for the better off, add detail to this evening scene, frozen in time at five to six by Big Ben, and with everyone heading for home as a slight mist begins to form over the river. Westminster Bridge, still at this time adorned with its beautiful gas lamps, was designed by Thomas Page and completed in 1862, replacing an earlier stone bridge. In 1910, which is the date for this painting, it had recently been strengthened, and the density of the road traffic shows the reason for this precaution. Now, over ninety years later, the splendid bridge is still doing well.

When looking at a painting it is all too easy to be mesmerised by the main object or objects portrayed. Look at the picture more closely at the less obvious, and the tricks of the trade will become apparent. For example a low mist is beginning to form over the Thames that not only gives depth to the bridge on the right-hand side of the picture but also separates the B-type bus from the base of Big Ben. The cluster of lights on the far side of the bridge is positioned such that the light reflected on the road and tram rails separates the wheels of the taxi and the near bus. Overall the colours are subdued so that when the lights are added they have punch.

Empire Flying Boat
Painted 2000

As passenger aircraft grew larger and heavier in the 1930s, length and strength of runways at airports became an increasing problem. For some designers the answer lay with aircraft that could take off and land on water. Seaplanes – aircraft fitted with floats instead of landing wheels – were already very successful. But for economical passenger and cargo operations something much larger was called for. The result was the development of the flying boat, and the largest and most remarkable of these were the Short Sunderland and the Saunders-Roe Princess.

In the 1930s Imperial Airways was the premier airline in the UK and when it was decided to pioneer a route to the east, Short Sunderland flying boats, which were given the name 'Empire Flying Boats' were used. The use of flying boats meant that ports like Alexandria and Basrah could be used as staging posts, without the need for elaborate airport facilities and long runways. Later in the 1930s British Overseas Airways also operated Empire Flying Boats for mail, as well as passengers and freight. The aircraft had two decks, and passengers were accommodated in a midships, promenade, and an aft cabin. It appears that about 20 passengers could be carried if a full load of freight was on board. Power was provided by four engines, though finding engines powerful enough was a problem.

In the late 1930s it was decided to run a transatlantic service, and air refuelling trials were undertaken with *Cabot*, the Empire Flying Boat shown in our picture. The aircraft was to have an additional 900 gallons of fuel pumped into it after it had taken off, over Southampton, and then to be refuelled again over Newfoundland. There is a photograph of refuelling from a Harrow tanker aircraft. The fuel hose is connected to the Empire's back end, but how was it done? Was there any improvement on the 'dangle and grab' method of 1923?

Barton's Coach
Painted 1996

There is supposed to be a spot somewhere south-east of Coventry which is furthest from the sea in England. It depends a bit on how you classify the Bristol Channel. For the English, as an island nation, accessibility to the sea has always been of great importance. The sea conjures up visions of sandcastles, paddling, learning to swim in the days before widespread municipal swimming pools, sailing boats, and eventually a ferry-crossing to lands beyond the horizon. There are stories of Drake, Cook and Nelson, and many others, whose exploits at sea have earned enduring fame. The sea means sparkling waters, cloudless skies and the cry of the seagulls, all evoked by this picture. Sadly, as many a day excursion found out, it was not always like that!

From early motoring days charabancs were perceived to be the answer for many people when it came to holiday travel, and our frontispiece records the scene early in the twentieth century. By the 1930s the coach as we know it was well established, and the Bedford seen third in line on Scarborough seafront, and also portrayed on page 79, is an example of a very popular and widespread model. By the 1950s larger and more streamline vehicles were the order of the day. A number of manufacturers produced coach chassis, among them Bedford, Albion, Atkinson, AEC, Ford and Leyland. Coach operators could then have bodies of their choice made by a number of coachbuilding companies such as Plaxton, Duple and Park Royal. The coach at the front, RAL 37, has a Plaxton Ventura style body set on a Leyland PS1 chassis. It is registered in Nottingham, where Barton's coaches were based. In 1955, the date of this picture, Barton's had a fleet of 138 double-decker and 148 single-decker vehicles. They must have needed a large car park when they were all at home!

Fowler Engine Threshing

Painted 2001

Harvesting has always been the climax of the farming year, and for many centuries corn was cut by hand, threshed with flails, and winnowed with a shovel. Over two hundred years ago primitive threshing machines were invented, wind and water powered, or by horses. The corn might have to be taken some distance to the machine. The horse-propelled binder for reaping was invented in 1827 by Dr Patrick Bell. In our picture the three machines which revolutionised the harvesting process are depicted in about the year 1942, by which time the 1941 Fordson Model N tractor has been painted green for camouflage! The traction engine, built by John Fowler of Leeds, is a 7hp model of 1907 vintage, so coming to the end of its working life. In future a tractor pulley would supply the power for many years derived from a steam engine.

The threshing machine shown at work is a Clayton & Shuttleworth model. The author remembers the distinctive undulating hum that could be heard miles across the countryside, drawing him like a magnet. The threshing team, consisting of traction engine or tractor, threshing machine and perhaps elevator, would travel from farm to farm and establish themselves in the rickyard. Corn might be brought directly from the field, as here, or might be already stacked in skilfully constructed ricks. Sheaves would be transferred to the top platform of the machine, the string cut, and they were fed into the threshing drum. The distinctive noise came from the fan used to winnow the grain. The corn was bagged into sacks as shown, while the straw, emerging from the other end of the machine, was carried up an elevator to the growing top of the straw stack. Half-a-dozen men or more would be required to keep the process running smoothly, which is a great contrast to the two men who can now harvest a large field using a combine harvester, in far less time. The modern procedure is also less at the mercy of the weather, as not all harvesting days were like the one pictured. Stooks in the field would suffer in quality if they got a soaking. Delving into memories of harvest time, it is a fair guess that the brown jar contained a pretty strong brew of something that was not tea!

Esso Super Pluto

Painted 2001

The work undertaken at airports is often so specialised that the vehicles used have to be of unusual design and capability. This is particularly true of the refuelling process for aircraft, where speed and, above all, safety are vital factors. The Foden S20 tanker which is the centrepiece of this painting was produced in the later 1950s, and was adapted from the standard Foden articulated tanker. The rounded standard cab was raised, and two extra windows fitted to give visibility upwards to help the driver manoeuvre around parked aircraft in safety. Extra spotlights were also fitted for night work, and the tanker could carry 6000 gallons of 145-octane aviation fuel, and pump this into an aircraft at approximately 50 gallons a minute. The hose used had an open-ended nozzle, which would not be considered a good idea today!

Foden was a company famous as vehicle builders, going back to traction engines in 1882. The first steam lorry was produced in 1900. By the late 1920s steam vehicles were at a disadvantage, and Foden reluctantly turned to producing diesel lorries, the first in 1931 being fitted with a Gardiner engine. Before the war Foden was producing a fine range of vehicles, including eight-wheel lorries and an eight-wheel tanker of very modern design. The Super Pluto, with its streamlined cab and body, and prominent 'Esso' markings was a worthy successor.

Behind the tanker can be seen the front of a Karrier box van of 1952 date. Karrier was a company under the Rootes Group umbrella, and the vehicles were built alongside the Commer range of vans and lorries. In the background can be seen the tail of a BOAC Vickers Vanguard, and on the right-hand side an older Starways Vickers Viking. The latter is the aircraft receiving refreshment from Pluto!

What Seems to be the Trouble?

Painted 1994

The Morris 8 Series E has struggled up the long steep hill until nearly at the top of Kirkstone Pass, west of Penrith in present-day Cumbria, and there has gently died. Going up such hills in the small cars of the 1930s and 40s was always a considerable adventure, with the necessity of double de-clutching down into the lowest gear – never easy to achieve on the move, and the possibility of being blocked by a stalled car in front. Handbrakes were notoriously unreliable also. One reached the top with a great sense of achievement and relief, only to be suddenly aware, with a sinking feeling, that where you had come up you would almost certainly have to go down, and if engines were inclined to be unreliable, brakes could be even more so. In deepest Devon passengers often had to walk up hills to help the little Hillman Minx, and sometimes they preferred to walk down the hills as well!

In this case the little pool of oil just visible under the engine suggests that the effort has been too much. Probably an oil seal has failed. The expressions on the faces of the three chief participants tell the rest of the story. The AA patrol-man is inspecting the scene of the disaster with cool professionalism. He happened to be passing at the right moment and spotted a member in distress. But whether he can sort this problem out by the roadside is uncertain. Meanwhile his hands remain behind his back! The owner of the car, a few minutes ago exulting in the triumph of climbing the long hill unscathed, is now reduced to a nervous near-wreck, full of apprehension. His wife, on the other hand, is sitting quite unconcerned, door open into the road, drinking a cup of tea and leaving it all to the menfolk to sort out.

The Automobile Association was founded in 1905, to offer help to motorists in a variety of ways. The first motor-cycle combination was introduced in 1920, and in the following years Chater-Lea and Triumph motorcycles were used. Later BSA combinations were introduced, and the AA took delivery of their 1000th model in 1947. The BSA 600 M21 shown in the picture was introduced in the early 1950s. The patrolman could give members up to one hour's assistance by the roadside, but if that was not possible an AA-appointed garage could also give an hour's work paid for by the AA. Mini-van patrols were introduced in 1962, and the last motorcycle combination was decommissioned in 1968.

Cadbury's Van

Painted 2000

For one young gentleman paradise is a small shop on a corner in the backstreets of his home town, where he can press his nose against the window and mentally sample the contents of the two rows of glass jars so invitingly displayed! It is the months before the outbreak of the Second World War, with the consequent introduction of that greatest of all horrors for children, sweet rationing.

Our young customer has yet to worry about ration books; his only concern is financial. How much of what can he buy with the few pence of pocket money jingling in his pocket? Meanwhile fresh supplies are coming in, and there may even be something he has not tried before.

The route from the factory at Bournville to the customer's mouth involves carefully packed boxes, and the latest model of Bedford KV van, first introduced by Bedford in 1939, and built at their Luton factory. It was a much more elegant and streamlined version compared to its predecessors of the early 1930s. Powered by a six-cylinder petrol engine rated at 27hp it had plenty of power, and was designed for 30 and 40cwt payloads. The vehicle shown is the 30cwt van, and Cadbury's operated a fleet of these popular vans. Production was curtailed by the war, and Bedford contributed 250 000 vehicles to the War Department. After the war the popular 1939 models were continued until they were superseded in the 1950s.

Chocolate bars were first invented by Joseph Fry in the late-eighteenth century. The firm of Cadbury was founded in 1831 by John Cadbury, producing cocoa products in an old malthouse in Crooked Lane, Birmingham. John Cadbury handed the business over to his sons, Richard and George, who like him were also members of the Society of Friends, and it was their vision which led to the purchase of 14 acres of land south of Birmingham in 1878, and the building of the Bourneville factory and community. The site had an excellent road, canal and rail links, and a good water supply. The company continued to develop throughout the twentieth century, keeping faith with its founders, and always being in the forefront of care for workers and their conditions of work, while producing very tasty chocolate!

BR Scammell Scarab

Painted 1995

This evocative scene is a reminder of the close links between road and rail in the days before all the branch lines were closed, and freight had to take entirely to the roads, in a move detrimental to our national transport system ever since. Every small town would have its goods depot, even if it could only accommodate a couple of wagons, as is the case here, and there was a loading bay where flat trucks or box vans could unload and load direct from the railway wagons. The distance of just a few feet between each meant labour was kept to a minimum. Space could be quite restricted, however, and this is where the Scammell Scarab came into its own. By using a three-wheel tractor, coupled to an articulated trailer of modest size, Scammell created a vehicle which was almost able to turn round in its own length. It was so versatile in this respect that it earned the nickname 'Mechanical Horse'.

The Scarab, named after the beetle considered sacred by the ancient Egyptians, did have a certain resemblance at the front. The first 'Mechanical Horse' was introduced in 1932, and was developed as a result of Scammell's experience with articulated lorries. It soon revolutionised short-haul collection and delivery work for the four railway companies, while many municipal authorities used the refuse-collection version. After the war a more streamlined tractor unit was introduced, with updated trailers for different uses, and the model shown in our picture is again in use by British Railways. Its varied cargo shows how indispensable it was in providing the necessary feeder service for the trains. The author can remember 'Passenger Luggage in Advance' (PLA) items being collected and delivered by these lorries in the late 1940s, when home was seven miles from the station. The lorry seen behind the Scarab is a Ford Thames 2-ton flat truck, of the type introduced in 1939, also a very successful vehicle.

One of the earliest Dinky Toy models was a 'Mechanical Horse', and an article in the *Meccano Magazine* of 1936 gave full instructions for the younger generation on how to couple up the tractor and trailer just like the real one. The models were produced also in the livery of the four main railway companies, as well as some other ones, and different trailers were available.

King George V leaving Oban
Painted 1998

There is a certain magic where the land meets the sea, where train or car gives place to ship, and it is captured beautifully in this scene where the train rests by the quay, and the engine's smoke mingles with that of the stately steamer slowly and majestically moving out. It reminds one again of the seagulls' cry, sunshine and sea, and holidays. The steamer *King George V* is shown leaving Oban, situated at the east end of the Firth of Lorn in Argyll, Scotland, and from this port the David McBrayne steamers serve the routes to many of the western islands off the north-west coast of Scotland. Our picture shows a sunny and calm day, but it is not often like that!

The steamer *King George V* was launched in 1926, and was of 815 tons gross. She was 270-feet long, and with a beam of 32 feet. Powered by two steam turbines, she had a top speed of 16 knots. She had plenty of open deck space for passengers to enjoy the magnificent views on sunny days, and with her wooden bridge superstructure and twin red funnels, she was a very smart ship indeed, and a credit to 'McBraynes of the Highlands'. She was eventually taken out of service after a long life, and having successfully avoided any collisions with the many hazards to be found in the west Scottish seas.

Sometimes the railway companies ran their own steamer services, as with the Great Western Railway services from Fishguard to Ireland, and from Weymouth to the Channel Islands. The locomotive in the picture being rather eclipsed by the steamer is a McIntosh Caledonian 439 also known as a Standard Passenger Class loco. This 0-4-4-T locomotive was introduced in 1900, so had already seen plenty of service before *King George V* was launched.

Panther Motorcycle
Painted 1997

It was fun trying to date the scene in this picture. The three vehicles date from the mid 1930s, and the most significant feature is the lack of traffic, allowing the two friends to block the road completely as they stop for a chat. This seems to indicate a time of fuel rationing, and one suspects engines have been turned off, both to make a conversation possible, and to prevent consumption of precious petrol! The fact that the iron railings have not been cut off and taken away to be made into Spitfires may not be significant, as the artist knows of some that survived this fate. The registration number on the car indicates London, so the venue could be anywhere in outer London.

The Ford Popular 8hp saloon, (Model Y) was introduced in 1933, and advertised as 'The £100 Ford saloon'. A picture showed one family, snug in the car, cruising past another envious family waiting at a bus stop – a reversal of the transport propaganda of today! The Ford Y was an ultra-basic car, in keeping with its low price, but it made cars affordable for many, and other companies like Morris were forced to follow suit rapidly. The Ford was a worthy successor to the Model T.

Panther motorcycles were also made from the mid 1930s, and were notable for their long-stroke 500cc engines, with the cylinder set at an angle tilting forward. Because of the design, the four-stroke engine was a good 'slogger', and popular with those who fitted sidecars to increase the capacity of the family transport. The Panther was very much on a par with other makes such as Triumph, Ariel, Norton and BSA.

In the background a Morris Post Office van delivers the mail – reminding the author of one of his first Dinky Toy models.

A photograph taken over half a century ago of my grandfather proudly posing with his Panther motorcycle formed the basis of this painting. Although he died before I was born I would like to think that he would be proud to be remembered in this way. To complete the family scene I have also included the car that belonged to my other grandfather.

BRS Mammoth Major
Painted 1993

A wet day, and what a contrast in transport. The AEC Mammoth Major eight-wheel flatbed lorry carried a payload of up to 15 tons, and was powered by a six-cylinder 9.6-litre diesel engine. In those days before power steering the driver had to be fit as well as skilful, and the lorry drivers were always considered to be the best on the road, not least because of the courteous way they waved faster traffic past their plodding vehicles. How times have changed – one has a job to keep up with them today! The registration number is for Southampton, but as British Road Services covered the entire country, we could be anywhere.

The Ford 8hp Popular driving away from the level crossing was the post-war version of the 1939 Ford 'Eight', and the successor to the Model Y (page 38). Nicknamed the 'Sit-up-and-beg' Ford, because of its upright styling, it was again a basic little car, but robust, with an 8hp engine driving through a three-speed gearbox, and a top speed of about 55mph with the wind and tide! In the early 1950s a sidevalve engine of 1172cc was substituted, giving a higher speed and much reduced fuel consumption.

Like the lorry driver, the watching signalman also had to be fit, as opening and closing the crossing gates involved much spinning of his huge control wheel.

Off to the Coast
Painted 1997

The Royal Blue Coach Service always meant holidays. These smart and comfortable coaches were employed on long-distance routes, and it is likely that this one, though registered in Devon, will have started its journey to Swanage from a London terminus. It is mid-afternoon, by the shadows, so the timing would fit, though the gentleman sitting on the wall in front of the Bank's Arms seems to still be clutching the remains of a pint. The scene dates from the early 1950s, and the coach is a Duple-bodied 1951 Bristol LL6 B rated as a 37-seater. There is no difficulty about the place, for the ruins of Corfe Castle stand guard as ever over the route to Swanage and the sea.

In front of the Greyhound Hotel stands the 1947 version of the popular Hillman Minx, which was to be superseded by yet another Minx model in 1952. The sidevalve engine was rated at 1184cc, and drove through a four-speed gearbox. This model differed from the pre-war Minx in that it had a more wrap-round radiator grille, and an enlarged boot, which meant the flat back of the pre-war models was now replaced with a bulge, as seen in the picture. The rendered buildings, roofed with local slates, give a very mellow atmosphere to this lovely village on a sunny day.

Coal Lorry (Leyland Comet)
Painted 1995

What a contrast to the previous picture, but the necessities of life are just as important, and coal was a chief one! Amidst the cobbled streets, with their back-to-back houses, it is Monday, and the fires under the coppers have been lit at dawn. Now the task is well under way, and the washing is hung out to dry. One cannot but feel that even if the housewife is lucky and avoids passing showers, her washing is fighting a losing battle against smoke from the factory chimneys and passing trains on the railway line, not to mention dust from the coal lorry doing the deliveries! Her neighbour, meanwhile, has laid out a rug to air on her front fence, no doubt having shaken and beaten it well first.

The coal merchant would operate out of a yard, often sited beside the railway line which brought him his supplies straight from the mines. Here he would bag the fuel into different categories – house coal, anthracite and coke – to deliver to houses. Cellars and bunkers would accommodate the different types of fuel to ensure that domestic boilers, open fires and coppers would all run efficiently. Like others, the coalman had to be fit, for his much-used sacks weighed in at 1cwt, and he would shift many hundreds in a day. No wonder he tended to heave them into household bunkers as quickly as possible, oblivious to the dust he was causing to fly about on washing day.

The coalman's vital transport is a flatbed Leyland Comet, introduced by Leyland in 1947, and featuring a semi-forward-control cab. This popular lorry was not superseded until 1960. Behind it, one of the railway arches has been filled in, and the 'Shell' advertisement, and oil drums, indicate that the resulting space is being used for some variety of very basic car repairs or the like. Another advertisement suggests 'Virol for those who are flagging!'

The mere mention of Leyland Comet and my thoughts go back to Christmas morning some time in the late 1950s. There were toys, and special toys – the latter being ones that you knew cost a lot of money and had to be looked after. Victory Industries, I believe of Guildford, produced a series of cars and the Leyland lorry. They were large scale, very accurate for the time and were driven by an electric motor. The plastic bodies, metal fittings, and treaded rubber tyres made them a joy to behold. I still have the Comet to this day and every time I see it I am reminded of the hundreds of tight circles that it travelled around my grandmother's chair leg that Christmas.

Country Picnic
Painted 1995

This nostalgic scene is a reminder of the days when one could open a gate and pull off the narrow country lane into a harvested hay field for a picnic, and relax while being fortified with the contents of a well-equipped picnic basket, while the children kicked a ball about to work off surplus energy before being confined in the car again. The sun, it seems, always shone, and there were never unwelcome visitors like wasps to the feast! In fact, such freedom was based on a mutual trust between farmer and travellers. Because the latter did not leave gates open, damage growing crops, or leave the place strewn with litter, the farmer had no need to threaten prosecution or chase them away with dogs. Today people march to demand freedom of access to the countryside, without considering that it has been the irresponsibility and even vandalism of the public that has put farmers and landowners on the defensive.

But all is peaceful here, and the gleaming car which is the instrument of such freedom, looks brand spanking new. If it is, then the date is 1948, and petrol is still in short supply. So are cars, so our father of the family might well smoke a pipe and look self-satisfied. Triumph had by this time been taken under the Standard umbrella, three years before, and the new Triumph Renown saloon, with its very distinctive styling, was powered by the Standard Vanguard engine, with four cylinders rated at 2088cc. With a maximum speed just below 80mph, this was an elegant car with a good performance.

Pionair Leopard
Painted 1999

In 1933 the new Douglas DC1 amazed the aeronautical world with its revolutionary design based on retractable undercarriage, controllable propeller and new conception of the use of flaps. The Douglas DC3, known as the Dakota, was introduced in 1935, and was a remarkable development of the earlier aircraft. In fact it must be one of the most successful aircraft ever to fly, in both peacetime and wartime conditions. During the war it undertook a wide variety of tasks, especially ferrying passengers and cargo. However, it was peacetime operations flying for a large number of airlines which made the aircraft so famous, as it became the mainstay of many shorter domestic routes.

By 1955 the DC3 could claim to be the most widely used transport in the world, 10 926 of the aircraft having been built. Of these 10 123 were built as military transports, and many of these were then converted for civilian use after the war. Some were powered by two Wright Cyclone GR 1820 engines, developing 1100hp each, others by 1200hp Pratt & Whitney Twin Wasp 1830–92 engines. The DC3 had a maximum speed of 216mph and a cruising speed of 167mph. It was a very handy aircraft, and the author remembers the ease of a flight from London to Orkney in 1955, with stops at Birmingham, Edinburgh, Aberdeen and Wick. This was undertaken in a British European Airways Pionair Leopard which was the name given to the DC3 by that airline. The aircraft in our picture is named *Sir Henry Royce*, after the great car and aircraft pioneer, and is also engaged in carrying mails. The earlier Pionair had integral steps in the drop-down passenger door. The later Pionair had new instruments and radio, making the presence of a radio operator unnecessary, and thus the crew was reduced to two, while the aircraft carried 32 passengers. It had an enlarged freight door, and needed separate steps when configured for passenger operation.

BP Tanker

Painted 1994

Before the Second World War there was much competition between the petrol companies, with advertisements like 'That was Shell, that was…' and even ditties like 'Teeny weeny motors may, pass much bigger cars than they, if they'll only learn to say, use BP!' The war, with the introduction of 'pool petrol' put an end to the competition, and the beleaguered motorist was glad for every drop of fuel he could get, of whatever variety. Petrol was distributed to garages from the nearest refinery, and after the war there is evidence that the oil companies continued what was the most efficient means of operation, whatever the labels on the pumps said. In the early 1950s the author's father carried out extensive tests on his new Jowett Javelin and established to his own satisfaction that it gave its best performance using 'National Benzole Mixture'. There were sometimes problems finding a garage with the right brew but with hindsight it seems that that they might all have been the same anyway!

In our picture there is a mixture as well, with a Shell-Mex and BP tanker passing a garage stocking just BP petrol. The driver has stopped to have a word with the forecourt attendant, who is whiling away the time without a customer by sweeping up. He appears to be saying, 'None today, thank you.' The petrol tanker is a Commer 12-ton TS3 lorry capable of carrying 2000 gallons of petrol. The scene is set in about the mid 1950s, and by this time Commer had been part of the Rootes group for many years.

The Vauxhall 10/4 saloon is of 1938 vintage, but looks very well preserved, perhaps because like many cars it was laid up throughout the war. It does have a dent in the front bumper, but then what were bumpers for? This popular family saloon was powered by a 1442cc ohv engine, and was produced both before and after the war. The car hails from West Suffolk, while the tanker dwarfing it is registered in London. The unusual church tower is typical of Suffolk, while the well-remembered adverts on the wall complete a picture full of detail.

Moy's Cart
Painted 1998

Looking back, the horse and cart had many advantages for short-distance urban deliveries: quiet and economical, more or less free from noxious emissions, easy to park, distinctive as an advertisement, and liable to leave a helpful contribution to the welfare of the rose bed!

Like the coalman on page 45, this employee of Moy's, a well-known supplier of domestic fuels, operates out of a coal yard adjacent to the railway which brings in his supplies, and also is well used to heaving 1cwt bags about. The horse and cart was used by breweries and milkmen up to comparatively recent times, and there are still breweries like Adnams which have horse-drawn drays.

The cart in use here is a flatbed model with turning front wheels and leaf springs on both sets of wheels, quite a modern luxury! The wood-spoked wheels have hardly changed down the centuries. Horse-drawn carts of various types have been used for thousands of years, one of the earliest being the war chariot. Hundreds of different varieties have been developed, from the small two-wheel farm cart to the gold coronation coach! Looking back it is truly amazing how horse-drawn transport could be adapted for such a variety of uses.

In this picture an actual location is portrayed, and the factory with the chimney is Cocksedges of Halstead, in Essex, who specialised in wood turning, and made balls for coconut shies, skittles, polo balls etc. Sadly, the picture is very much a portrait of a bygone age.

Three Minis
Painted 1997

The manufacturers of small cars often organise the size of their smaller cars to go in cycles. Thus Austin began with the Austin 7 Chummy in 1923. Throughout the 1920s and 30s the Austin 7 grew progressively larger, as Ruby succeeded Box Saloon, and finally came the 1938 7.99hp Big Seven, which was really an Eight! After the war the sizes increased until the introduction of the Austin A30 in 1951, hailed in advertisements as the 'New Austin 7'. This little car was developed through the 1950s, became the A35, then the A40 Farina. But people still wanted an Austin 7, and in 1959 Alec Issigonis came up with the Austin Mini. By this time the British Motor Corporation was in being, and the Mini became the smallest car in the range for both Austin and Morris, replacing the Austin A35/40, and the Morris Minor.

The Mini was distinctive in being a small body shell, with four small wheels set at each corner. Add a transverse-mounted engine and front-wheel drive, and the result was a car with a remarkable amount of room inside for its overall size, excellent performance and superb road-holding qualities, soon demonstrated in racing and rallying. Different engine sizes and fine tuning gave a top speed in excess of 100mph and fuel consumption could be as much as 70mpg, depending on how fast you drove. For a time the Mini cost less than £500 in its basic form, and was therefore within the reach of thousands of motorists. With the introduction of a new Mini in the last couple of years, it looks as though the Mini may become one of the longest-running models, even threatening the Volkswagen!

In this highly nostalgic view of the 1960s we see the Austin and Morris Minis parked outside the local cinema on a Saturday night, while boy meets girl – the latter also in a mini (skirt) though they were to go much shorter than this! The Queen's Jubilee events were a reminder of how timeless the music of the Beatles has proved to be, as also are the James Bond films. Next week our picture promises 'Twice as much Elvis as ever', as well as the possibility of parking right outside the front doors as these were the days before double-yellow lines!

The brief for this picture was transport in the 1960s and I can think of no better way to represent this than the Beatles and the Mini (cars and skirts!). A local cinema, albeit now a multiscreen, provided the backdrop. The choice of Mini came as a result of luck, fate, call it what you will. On my way home from the cinema where I had taken photographs I followed this very 1963 Mini to my home town. I there asked the young lady to whom the car belonged if I could also photograph her Mini. She was very happy for me to do so but must have wondered why I had followed her!

Cook's Van

Painted 1991

This scene, showing Halstead, Essex in the 1930s, is typical of many a town in that period. The High Street, with its wide variety of shops catering for every need is served by delivery vans like the Dennis van which kept the shops well stocked. Meanwhile the potential customers could drive into town in their comfortable cars like the saloon shown, park right outside the shop of their choice, and go in search of saucepan or hat or whatever, without someone in a black-and-yellow cap – wasp colours – leaping out of ambush and spoiling the day with a parking ticket! It is an everyday scene of the period, but the essence of an English town is portrayed here, and should be a constant reminder of how precious our local High Street is today, and should be in the future.

Cook's started brewing in 1885, and their fine ales proved so popular that they moved several times to larger premises, and had to replace their horse-drawn carts eventually with a fleet of motor lorries in 1925. Two of these were Dennis vans, and one of these is shown number VX577, an Essex registration. This is a Dennis 30cwt van, introduced in 1925, and continuing in production until 1933. It was powered by a four-cylinder 17.9hp engine, through a three-speed gearbox, later replaced by a four-speed one, and had rear-wheel mechanical brakes, plus a brake on the transmission. When fully laden, travelling downhill required care and lowest gear!

The unusual saloon car parked in front of London House, the emporium of Simmons Bros, Draper and Milliner, is an Austin 16 of mid-1930s' vintage.

Mauretania

Painted 1999

This is a wonderful portrait of one of the greatest liners ever to sail the high seas. Samuel Cunard founded the Cunard Line in 1840. During the next sixty years about 25 ships from *Britannia* to the *Umbria* and *Campania* followed one another, establishing Cunard as the leading shipping line on the North Atlantic route. By the beginning of the twentieth century the demand was so great, and technology so improved, that Cunard, with government aid, commissioned two new liners, the *Lusitania* and the *Mauretania* which went into service in 1907. Tragically the *Lusitania* was sunk by a German submarine off Ireland during the early months of the First World War, with over 1000 lives lost.

The *Mauretania* was a ship of 32 000 tons, propelled by four direct-driven steam turbines which were coal fired in the early days. It was a daunting job for the stokers, each having to lift 5 tons a day of the 7000 tons of coal the liner carried to feed the 192 furnaces heating 25 boilers. It was such hot work the men only did twenty-one-minute spells. After the war she was converted to oil burning, and the stokers' ghastly job was at an end. The *Mauretania* was designed to do 24½ knots, but she comfortably exceeded that speed, and easily captured the Blue Riband of the Atlantic on her first voyage, and held it for an incredible twenty-two years until 1929. During her last years she was used as a cruise ship, often to the Mediterranean, and eventually she left New York for the last time on 26 September 1934, with many sad farewells. That same day the *Queen Mary* was launched.

The *Mauretania* will always represent a milestone not only in transatlantic travel, but also in the maritime history and achievement of Great Britain.

I seem to recall the weather on the days that followed the Nostradamus prediction of 'the end of the world' being very turbulent. Skies threatened and storms raged – not to mention the tornadoes in the Midlands. One of these storms was captured on camera from our bedroom window for future pictorial use, in this case the Mauretania. Maritime scenes with large areas of uninterrupted sky lend themselves well to the threat of the elements. As the ship passes through brief sunlight, will it bypass the storm?

Ferguson Tractor

Painted 1995

What a contrast to the threshing team of the war years (page 27), with plenty of manpower needed to assist the machinery. Now in the early 1960s two men undertake the entire harvest, with the help of two machines, and later a bailer. Massey Harris was an old-established maker of farm implements, dating back to the 1930s. It produced a developing range of machinery, including tractor-drawn binders, and was a pioneer in the combine harvester's progress. In 1957 Massey Harris merged with Ferguson, and the combine shown in this painting is a 780 model dating from 1958. It has a 10-foot pickup reel, with attachments for other crops such as grass and peas, and could be powered either by a six-cylinder Austin petrol/paraffin engine or a Perkins' diesel. The cost was around £500 new!

The Ferguson story begins in the early 1930s, when Harry Ferguson, who was a brilliant inventor, devised a three-point attachment for implements on the back of a tractor. Ferguson at first teamed up with David Brown, who made tractors, and the first model was the 'Black Tractor' of 1933. The Ferguson-Brown company floundered in the difficult economic conditions, and in 1938 Ferguson gave a remarkable demonstration to Henry Ford of his tractors' abilities. In June 1939 the first was produced, and within a year 10 000 had been sold.

In 1946 Ford and Ferguson split up, rather unhappily, and Harry Ferguson set up his own plant in the UK to produce his tractors. His first model, produced in 1947, was the Ferguson TE-20, known to many as the Grey Fergie. This versatile little tractor, with its integral implements, economical performance and great manoeuvrability proved to be a great favourite with farmers, market gardeners and smallholders. It was easy to drive – the author started his driving career on one – and had the usual hand-throttle, footbrakes and clutch. An unusual feature was the use of the gear lever to activate the starter motor, so that the engine could not be started when one was in gear, a clever safety feature.

Sometimes one can spend vast amounts of time searching for suitable subjects for paintings, especially unproductive if working to a schedule. Conversely a scene sometimes presents itself most unexpectedly, and such was the case with this picture. I was a few miles from home on a glorious day when I passed a field of corn ripe for harvesting complete with old combine harvester. I spoke to the extremely co-operative driver and said that it would make a good picture if a Ferguson TE-20 was added, to which he replied, 'We have one of those too!'

A Tight Fit

Painted 2001

Was the bus built to fit the arch or vice versa? Actually, the archway looks much the older, but it must be rare to have vehicles specially shaped to fit a bridge under which they need to pass. Here AEC double-decker no. 644 passes through Beverley Bar in order to enter the centre of Beverley in East Yorkshire. The year is 1961, and the bus, owned by East Yorkshire Motor Services, is working the route from Scarborough to Hull on a very wet day. It looks like winter, too, as part of the bus radiator has been blanked off in an attempt to keep the engine temperature higher. East Yorkshire can be a very chilly part of the world at times. One has to feel respect for the driver, for in spite of his specially shaped roof he had to be quite a good shot to put his bus through the arch at dead centre. One must also feel admiration for any passengers who sat on the top deck in the front seats – always the author's favourite spot if it was available! Not all drivers of double-decker buses have coped with low bridges so well.

A few miles north of Hull, Beverley is particularly noted for its fine minster founded by St John of Beverley, Bishop of York in about AD690. Thanks to Danish raids, a fire and a collapsing tower, the present building is the fourth church to be built, dating from about 1400. With twin towers, and an interior 332-feet long, it is an imposing building, filled with beautiful stone and wood carvings which are a timeless tribute to medieval craftsmanship. Beverley was once a fully walled town, but now only one of the five original fifteenth-century gates survives to test the skill of bus drivers. With its Guildhall, Georgian houses and market cross, it is well worth a bus trip.

Moving Day
Painted 1993

Other people's removals are always a source of great fascination to the neighbours, and the housewife in the foreground has so far taken ten minutes to put out her third milk bottle, and each has been brought separately! Furniture in those days of the later 1930s was mostly less bulky, especially in the smaller houses, so that the Guy removals van has been quite capable of managing the whole operation with the help of a porter's trolley for the more restricted work. The registration of the van is a Glasgow number, so we can conclude we are north of the border, as Callender is some miles north-west of Stirling.

The removals van is a Guy Vixen, introduced in 1934, and this model has the new radiator cap which featured a Native American's head with full head-dress. The van was produced with a number of different bodies, rated as capable of a 3-ton payload, and powered by a four-cylinder 22.5hp engine. The Guy company was founded by Sydney Guy in 1914, and for the next forty-seven years produced a range of distinctive and dependable commercial vehicles. In 1961 the company was acquired by Jaguar cars, and then in 1966 became part of BMC. In 1968 it all became Leyland Motors, and the Guy models disappeared in favour of the Leyland vehicles, another example of the 'Biggest is best' philosophy.

Behind the removals lorry can be seen the front of a Morris 8/5cwt van, of the type introduced in 1937, which was a very popular van for local deliveries by grocers, bakers and others.

Ex Mayor
Painted 2000

This wonderful painting captures all the excitement and mystique of the real funfair, as well as reminding one of the source of power which made the travelling entertainment possible in the first place. The 'Ex Mayor' Showman's engine, here owned by T. Tuby & Sons, could be used to move caravans about on site, but more important was the supply of electric power from its steam-driven generator for the festooned coloured lights, as well as the motors driving roundabouts and dodgem cars. When the day came for the fair to move on to its next venue, which could be quite a distance away, then the Showman's engine pulled a veritable train of wagons containing all the equipment (see page 97). This impressive machine was indeed a maid of all work.

The beautiful Showman's engine in the picture was built by Burrell of Thetford, one of the most famous of the traction engine builders. 'Ex Mayor' was built in 1925, and had a nominal horsepower of 10, which when one looks at the massive engine must have been very nominal! The engine was of a double-crank compound design, made especially for use as a road locomotive. However, it also featured a small power-driven crane mounted on the back which could be used for lifting equipment into place, thus demonstrating another talent of this versatile machine.

By the later 1940s most of these majestic engines had been replaced by purpose-built tractors, like that produced by Scammell, which also carried large generators. But for looks 'Ex Mayor' had them beaten every time!

Cars by Air

Painted 1995

It seemed a miracle that the Bristol 170 freighter, loaded with three cars and 18 passengers (the author's Land Rover carried seven!) and its crew ever got into the air, let alone stayed there for twenty minutes. A number of routes were used, Lympne in Kent to Le Touquet being the most popular because it was the shortest, but flights also left from Southend as shown in our picture. The freighter was rather noisy and not very comfortable, but it was efficient and an excellent way to cross the Channel if one did not fancy a rolling ferry. Bristol's 170 freighter, powered by two of the company's Hercules engines, was introduced in 1945, and service was launched in 1948, carrying two cars and eight passengers. The fare for a car and four passengers was £32 one way – perhaps they were not sure whether people would want to repeat the experience! In April 1953 the Bristol Super Freighter came into service, and this is the aircraft the author remembers, carrying three cars and up to 20 passengers. The Land Rover's headroom made it a tight squeeze, and that was before the addition of roof-rack luggage.

The Triumph Mayflower in the foreground has survived the flying experience and is heading for home, according to its registration number. The Mayflower was introduced in 1949 by Triumph, now a part of the Standard Motor Company, and had a 1247cc engine developing 38bhp. Like its big sister, the Renown (see page 47), it had distinctive 'razor's edge' styling, but perhaps because it competed with the Standard saloons it was discontinued after a few years, leaving the Renown alone. An Austin Devon (see page 105) can be seen being reversed down the aircraft ramp by one of the airline employees, and behind the ramp can be glimpsed an AEC Matador refuelling tanker.

Steamroller

Painted 1993

A whole variety of transport is portrayed in this rainy early-evening scene, including Shanks's pony – and notice the fur-lined, zip-up boots which were a speciality of the time! The oldest campaigners in the picture are the distant 0-6-0 J.15 tender engine doing a bit of shunting, and the star of the show, the Aveling & Porter Steamroller. This company was based at Rochester and built steamrollers from the early years of the twentieth century until the mid 1930s when it moved to Grantham. It then produced diesel-powered rollers under the name Aveling Barford. Illustrated here is a 10-ton Type F double-crank compound engine dating from about 1922, and registered in Essex. Steamrollers were often owned by private contractors, as well as by county councils, and they would not only tow a water trailer but often a caravan for the driver, and perhaps a long-suffering wife, to live in when working away from home.

Two cars are being held up while the steamroller effects repairs to the road. Behind the roller is a 1937 Morris 8 Series 2 saloon, still giving good service in the 1950s, nearly twenty years on. They were well-built little cars, witnessed by the number still on the roads today.

In 1956 the Austin A30 was upgraded by the manufacturers to the more powerful A35 with a 948cc engine. Introduced at the Earls Court Motor Show in 1951, the A30 shown had a chrome front-radiator grille, semaphore-type indicators, and a smaller rear window than the A35. With careful tuning it would go surprisingly fast, yet as a family car would carry four people and their luggage quite happily. A completely new four-cylinder ohv engine was developed for the A30 and this was the first BMC A-series engine which went on to power Minis and the Metro. It was of 803cc capacity, with a single Zenith carburettor, and drive through a four-speed gearbox, its total weight being only 13cwt, which all added up to a good, economical performance. Described as 'a very economical and practical car to run, but with real character' it has lasted very well, and the author has a lot of fun driving the later A35 almost every day.

Topping Up the Cellar
Painted 1994

Is it just coincidence that five of this collection of pictures depict ale in transit, or does it suggest something about our artist? Could it be that a long-ago encounter with the 'pub with no beer' has left its indelible mark? Perhaps appropriately, this was the first of Malcolm's pictures ever seen by the author, who was immediately hooked! The detail of the scene, depicting the everyday activities of one's own boyhood period, a time of being able to recognise every vehicle on the road, made a strong appeal, quite apart from the quality of the painting in every respect. Here the scene is set in rural Cambridgeshire, in the area served by the Greene King Brewery in Bury St Edmunds, Suffolk. This is a well-known local brewery which has deservedly grown over the years, and celebrated its bicentenary in 1999.

The Morris Commercial lorry which is bringing in the vital supplies is a 30cwt flat truck introduced in the later 1930s, and powered by a 2.5-litre petrol engine. It was quite a challenging vehicle to drive, with a tricky gearbox and rather heavy steering for its size. It was, however, an extremely reliable and economical lorry, and much used by many smaller businesses for local work. By this time Morris had taken over the Wolseley company, and the lorries were built at the company's factory at Adderley Park, Birmingham.

Cruising past, perhaps with the driver making a mental note that new supplies have arrived at the Dog and Duck, is a smart red MG Midget TC of 1949 vintage. This model had the distinctive cut away front wings, and was powered by a 2.5-litre engine, giving a spirited performance which could be really enjoyed before the days of speed cameras. There is nothing in the motoring world that feels so enchanting as an open tourer on a sunny day.

In some pictures I think it necessary to include human interest to further the story behind the picture, as is the case here where draymen unload the delivery lorry while a gentleman relaxes in the sun with his pint. A photograph of the pub was taken, the Morris Commercial added, and as for the gentleman on the seat he is my wife's uncle who kindly posed on a bench in our back garden. Ironically, he only rarely drinks!

Euston Taxi

Painted 1994

It is hard to imagine a greater contrast to the previous picture! Outside Euston Station, London, on an extremely wet night, the gentleman waving a rolled-up newspaper is relieved to see a taxi with its sign illuminated, indicating it is for hire, even if it is one of the older models.

The horse-drawn hansom cab was introduced in 1836, and the last one was withdrawn from service in 1947. The cab was so much a part of London life that it even inspired jokes, such as, 'Porter, call me a hansom cab!' 'Certainly sir. You are a hansom cab.' Not all that funny now, perhaps, but of their era. It was a natural development from the hansom cab to the motorised cab, and by 1905 the latter and the four-wheel Growlers were vanishing from the streets of London at the rate of 600 a year. In the period between 1900 and the outbreak of war in 1914, there was much competition between British, French and Italian motor manufacturers, and some unusual designs appeared. Austin were on the scene as early as 1906.

The cab being hailed by our damp traveller is the Austin LL (Low Loader) model of 1934, which gave wonderful service for many years on the streets of London. Behind and to the left can be seen the Austin FX3 cab of 1949 (see page 17). On the right, behind the man, is a Hillman Minx saloon from the late 1930s.

The London taxi drivers were, and still are, justly renowned for their knowledge of London, said to be learnt by riding round all the streets on bicycles, and could be relied upon to come up with some amazing routes to avoid bad traffic. They also had a daring disregard for other traffic, a habit not always appreciated by other road users. The author remembers, however, in 1953, that they gave the Land Rover driven by his mother a very wide berth! The Euston Doric arch in the background, sadly, was demolished in the 1960s when the station was rebuilt.

Stena Discovery

Painted 1998

It is an amazing experience, especially for a small-boat enthusiast, to cruise across the North Sea on the Stena Discovery at about 45mph and to look down on passing ships that seem to be becalmed, and like models on a boating lake! The Stena Discovery was built by Finnyards, in Finland, in 1997. She is a twin-hulled catamaran, with a gross tonnage of 19 638 tons. Her length is 127 metres, beam 40 metres, and her draught is 4.8 metres. She is designed to carry 375 cars or equivalent, together with 1500 passengers, all powered by four Wartsila Vasa engines, two with a kw/hp of gelm 2500 and two with gelm 1600. These engines propel the ship using water-jets, and the view astern when she is travelling at her full speed of 40 knots is awe-inspiring. The ship also has her water-jets so arranged that she is highly manoeuvrable when she is coming alongside a quay, being literally able to move sideways, a trick which many a motorist would love to emulate! The only time the ship blotted her copybook slightly was when she produced a wash which soaked all the tourists on Felixstowe beach! She regularly plies the run from Harwich to the Hook of Holland.

In the foreground of this painting can be seen one of the remaining Thames barges, *Hydrogen*, registered in London, and with her traditional tan sails furled on to their spars, ready to be quickly cast off when she gets under way. These ships have evolved over the centuries into unique flat-bottomed carriers, able to cope with shallow rivers or sail across the North Sea using detachable lee boards. Crewed only by a skipper and a mate, they carried every sort of cargo up and down the East Coast. At the end of the nineteenth century there were 2000 of them but by 1939 they had been scuppered by the arrival of the lorry, their numbers being reduced to just 600. Today the only survivor in its original condition is the *Cambria*, preserved by the Maritime Trust. *Hydrogen,* based at Ipswich docks, was built in 1907, with a steel hull, and is 95-feet long, with a beam of 22 feet. It was fascinating to go aboard her recently, and one cannot help wondering whether the Stena Discovery will last as long.

Summer Excursion
Painted 1993

Following this Eastern National coach up the steep hill must have been a great frustration for the driver of the Triumph Renown behind, who has been constantly changing from second to first gear all the way up, with all the necessary double de-clutching required. Now, with the coach driving down the middle of the narrow road, he still has no hope of overtaking even if the road ahead is straight and flat. You can almost hear him saying,'They've got no business to bring a coach up a road as narrow as this!' Meanwhile the coach passengers are having a wonderful mystery tour, and much enjoying the glorious scenery of the Yorkshire Dales. But an over-adventurous driver could end up in difficulties, and there is a tale of one coach that lost its way in the Devon lanes about this time, and found itself going down a rapidly narrowing lane which ended in a field! However, as we see, there are surprises of a different kind for the wandering coach, this one having been confronted at the top of the hill by a masked bandit brandishing a pistol, to the total unconcern of his older sister. One can almost smell the smoke from the caps – those little pink rolls with a brown blob of gunpowder at regular intervals – that were so noisily effective in the toy revolvers of the time, all now doubtless banned by Health and Safety rules!

The Bedford coach is a Duple-bodied OB. Introduced in the mid 1940s, it was a great favourite with bus and coach companies, and saw much service on local routes as well as excursions. Powered by a four-cylinder petrol engine rated at 26hp, it was usually a 27-seater. Although it was a pre-war design, it had pleasing lines, and continued in service all over the country for several decades. Eastern National took delivery of this coach in 1949, the same type, incidentally, which featured in the famous 1952 Ealing Comedy film *The Titfield Thunderbolt*, and which the crooks hoped would put the railway out of business.

The Triumph Renown was produced by Standard in 1948, and details of this attractive car are given on page 46.

Y.cpp, Line 374
lowed to copy
12 = 1670912, TRM_DATA_MODEl, block
0 (no read options)

.cpp, Line 3172
using DVD media

tCD.cpp, Line 245
ddress on media: 2147483646 (477218:
itten:

1670911 (371:18.61

Road Meets Rail

Painted 1997

The places where road met rail depended much on local geography and the views of local authorities and land-owners. In some towns, for instance in Devon, the railway station had to be sited in the valley, while the ancient town was perched on the nearby hill. In places such as Colchester and Newton Abbot the stations were quite removed from the town.

Brighton and Leicester, however, perhaps owing to a later date of main development, have their stations in the heart of the town. Certainly, as our picture shows, Southend Central Station is situated very close to the heart of town, as illustrated by the locomotive steaming over a teeming High Street into the station just to the left of the picture.

The scene is set in about 1950, with the road transport of either pre-war or early post-war vintage, and the 2-6-4 tank engine on the bridge carries the earlier British Railways roundel emblem on its side-tank, a lion atop one of the wheels. This three-cylinder tank engine, designed by Sir William Stanier for suburban passenger services, was first introduced in 1934. It was owned originally by the LMS (London, Midland & Scottish Railway), and later, after nationalisation, by the newly formed British Railways network. Its work was confined almost entirely to the LT & SR (London, Tilbury & Southend Railway) line between Fenchurch Street Station and Shoeburyness.

The painting also illustrates typical examples of bus, lorry and car. The British Railways lorry on the left waiting for a clear road is a 1950 3-ton Thorneycroft 'Nippy' lorry, much used for delivery work. Passing in front of it is an Austin 14hp Ascot saloon, which was first introduced in 1938, but also produced for a short time after the war. The double-decker bus heading for Shoebury Common is a brush-bodied Daimler CV, with a Lowbridge Utility body. This type was introduced between 1943 and 1945, and the vehicles were very faithful workhorses during the final years of the war. All these types of transport soldiered on through the 1950s.

UN 0, buffer 0x06343000
SCSI_ERR)
OK)
SCSI TASTATUS_CHKCOND)
DIUM_ERROR)

00 0x01 0xF4 0x00 0x00 0x00 0x20

03 0x00 0x00 0x00 0x0A
00 0x00 0x11 0x05

rv.cpp, Line 1442
UN 0, buffer 0x0611000

'THE AUSTIN A90 ASCOT
WAS NOT AVAILABLE
POST WAR —
THE POST WAR MODELS
WERE THE OHV 16 &
THE SIDE VALVE 12

Betterwear Van

Painted 1996

There are several mysteries surrounding this scene, which the artist does not seem able to explain! The time is the six years between 1933 and 1939, for the van is a Fordson, and the name was changed to Fordson Thames in 1939. It was the period when many deliveries were made to one's door, and they were things one actually wanted, from the butcher, baker, grocer and, in this case, the Betterwear man. We next have to note that although this Betterwear is not the company of a similar sounding name which supplies minor items of domestic equipment today, the side of the van says 'Brushes, Mops, Polishes'. But does the anticipation of the reception committee – a housewife in her apron, plus three dogs, one lurking further up the road – suggest something more exciting? The housewife is waiting by the open door, having heard the van arrive, and appears to be giving an instruction to the nearest dog, presumably to behave itself. Finally, the delivery man, having arrived in a 1½-ton van, is going through the gate with nothing more than a medium-sized suitcase. The question is, what is in the suitcase?

It may, of course, be a selection of dusters, or a new apron. Or could it be some 'better wear' of a much more exotic nature? Can we detect in her attitude of eager anticipation that this is a delivery she, and her husband, have been eagerly awaiting for several weeks? Will there be a trying-on session, and will the Betterwear man be called on to express an opinion? How long will he be detained by the farmer's wife, whose husband is out cutting the 20-acre field, and will the neighbours wonder why it takes him five times longer to make this call than any of the others on his round? The conclusion to all this is that we shall never know what that suitcase held, and rural life is never dull!

We can, at least, identify the van as a Fordson forward-control model as introduced in 1934. These larger vans were used for area deliveries by the Betterwear company, and then local agents used their own cars to visit customers. So again there is something unusual going on here!

One dog is a spaniel, and the other a Jack Russell, but the make of the third one up the road remains a further mystery!

National Service Return

Painted 1993

The young men newly returned from National Service have just disembarked from the P & O liner SS *Vienna*, which even when in service as a troopship would have given them a comfortable voyage and a fair amount of relaxation. Their next means of transport is the back of a Bedford QL, sitting on the wooden slatted seats along the sides, and being bounced about under the watchful eye of a member of the Royal Military Police. The Bedford QL 3-ton four-by-four was first introduced in the late 1930s, and was a forward-control design with the engine located between the driver and front passenger, making for warm winter conditions, and sweltering summer ones! The Army found the vehicle to be versatile, with ample space for cargo or personnel, and a good towing capacity especially when using the four-wheel drive over slippery or muddy rough ground. It was quite a challenge to drive, as the controls were basic, and the rather unresponsive engine coupled to a crash gearbox made gear changing a fine art. Any crashing of the gears would be greeted by loud cheering from the back, especially if the noise produced was loud enough to drown the lusty singing which helped to while away tedious and uncomfortable journeys.

The Bedford QL was replaced by the manufacturers with the Big Bedford 3-ton lorry of 1950, but the QL continued in service with the Army, and the ones driven by the author in the early 1960s were still in good form.

The SS *Vienna* was launched in 1929, and went into service with P & O in 1930. She was of 4326 tonnes gross, with a length of 366 feet and a beam of 50 feet; powered by two steam turbines, she could attain a speed of 19 knots. The ship was based at Harwich, and we see her tied up at Parkstone Quay. During the 1940s and 50s as a troopship she carried 1500 personnel but after National Service ended with the intake of January 1960, she was to make her last voyage as a troopship in July the same year.

Comet

Painted 1997

This striking picture, which is such a contrast of new and old, emphasises the astonishing beauty of the De Havilland Comet. The avoidance of engines hanging down beneath wings, or perched up on tails, together with the perfect line of the fuselage and the sweep of the wings, gave this aircraft a gracefulness seldom matched by any other. Because the Comet flew to South Africa, other artists have identified this as the perfect venue for a picture, but in this case Malcolm has been very careful to show the pyramids as they appeared in the mid 1950s, before Cairo had crept out to within a few hundred yards of the pyramids of Giza. There is not a tourist or a camel to be seen, but one can spot the small door by which one entered the pyramid.

The DH 106 Comet 1 entered service in 1952, being the logical development of the prototype which first flew on 27 July 1949. It was powered by four De Havilland Ghost turbojets, which in the Comet 2 were to be upgraded to Avon 503 turbojets of 7000lbs thrust. The Comet 1 accommodated up to 44 first-class passengers, and was designed for stage lengths of about 1750 miles; it could carry a payload of 13 000lbs, with a cruising speed of 480mph at 40 000 feet. This altitude factor contributed to the tragic crashes of three Comet airliners.

It is now suggested that because the Comet was developed and built as quickly as possible, and De Havilland insisted on using their less powerful Ghost engine, rather than the more powerful Rolls-Royce Avon, the weight of the aircraft had to be kept to a minimum. This meant the thinnest possible metal for the fuselage, and it is suggested that this, combined with the enormous pressure difference at an altitude of 40 000 feet contributed to the explosions that caused three Comets to crash. It was a great tragedy that the Comet, an aircraft so far ahead of any others in its day, should have been sabotaged by such an inbuilt flaw, and thus be denied the worldwide success it deserved. The aircraft's story also uncannily mirrors that of the airship R101, where again outside pressure was applied to hasten its introduction into service before full testing had been done.

Trolleybuses
Painted 1995

It is a cold winter's day, with slushy snow much in evidence, and no colder place to stand than at a bus stop in an exposed location. Even the bright red trolleybuses in this East London scene are hard put to it to make things look more cheerful, except that being inside will be a lot warmer than waiting at the bus stop! Trolleybuses, or 'trackless trolleys' as they were often called at first, were first introduced into this country in Bradford and Leeds in 1911. It was several years before they could be considered a reliable form of transport, but they were cheaper to install and maintain than trams, having no rails, and could use locally generated electricity such as had been provided for the trams they replaced. The single-decker models were soon replaced with double-deckers, obviously with a much increased passenger capacity. Being electrically powered they were environmentally friendly in urban areas, where lack of noise and fumes were a big bonus. There could be problems with the overhead wires; in winter ice would form on them, and at 'points' the pick-up could jump off the wire. The conductor on the trolleybus would carry a long pole with a hook, to catch the loop seen near the pick-up shoe, and replace the shoe on the wire. Then normal service could be resumed! There may have been disadvantages with the system, such as the restriction imposed by the wires, but the buses were a lot cleaner and quieter than the diesel buses which replaced them.

London Transport had a huge fleet of these trolleybuses, with a variety of body builders so that many of the vehicles were a mixture, and even more so when those which suffered bomb damage during the war were repaired by body builders other than those who made the original bodies. In this scene we see two vehicles, part of a fleet of this type of trolleybus which were delivered to London Transport in March 1938. The van just seen behind the bus appears to be a Morris, and the date would be early post-war.

Battle of Britain Harvest

Painted 1998

This powerful picture has a significant story to tell. In the air above, the Battle of Britain is raging, as seen by the twisting vapour trails, and the two Spitfires returning to refuel and rearm seem to be the nation's most precious commodity at this defining moment in history. Yet to our beleaguered nation, every ear of corn is just as precious in its way, and the land girl pitchforking the sheaves is intent on her work as her part in the conflict, leaving the fighters to take care of themselves. It is a very strong instinct, all the same, to stand and watch a pair of planes come safely in to land, especially when so many did not return, and when so much depended on them at this supreme moment of national tension.

The orange Fordson tractor is also noteworthy, for its plumage was to change colour abruptly in the near future. German fighter-pilots soon found that they could spot the colourful tractor miles away, and they took to strafing slow-moving tractors and their drivers as a safer option than taking on the Spitfires of the Royal Air Force. Not surprisingly, farmers rapidly found long-forgotten tins of green or brown paint, and the tractors sported a degree of camouflage which would have done credit to any unit in the armed forces! After the war the new Fordson tractor appeared in blue livery.

The N-type Fordson was first built at Cork, in Ireland, then manufacture was transferred to Dagenham in Essex in 1933, where production continued until 1945. Incidentally, this tractor was modelled as one of the first Dinky Toys in 1934.

Behind the tractor the corn sheaves are being loaded on to the back of a Ford Model B lorry, a wonderful general-purpose vehicle introduced in 1931, with size varying from 2 to 5 tons. Power was from either a four-cylinder 24hp engine, or a V8 developing 30hp. The summer of 1940 was a beautiful one, with long hot days, and this picture captures both the beauty and historical significance of those months of August and September 1940.

Snowdrift Rescue
Painted 1999

It is winter in the Scottish mountains, and the drivers and passengers of the Ford Anglia and the Leyland Comet are well and truly stuck in the snow which has drifted across the road. Their vehicles cannot be towed out at the moment, but it is some comfort to know that their plight has been spotted. The AA Dragon Rapide portrayed by Malcolm is a most interesting aircraft. It was released from military use in 1946, and acquired by Ind Coope, the brewers, who in turn passed it on to the Automobile Association in 1957. Based at Croydon Aerodrome, it was used to ferry senior AA staff, and also for traffic spotting, and on occasions such as the opening of the M1 motorway. As the winter of 1958 became increasingly severe in Scotland, the aircraft was moved north, to be used to spot people marooned in the snow, and to make supply drops from the air. It operated in AA colours only for six years, being replaced by the Association in 1963.

The De Havilland Dragon Rapide was first introduced in 1934, and between then and the end of production in 1946, a total of 697 aircraft were built. The aircraft had a maximum speed of 141mph and carried six passengers. The author flew in one from Bembridge on the Isle of Wight a few years ago, and remembers the adventure well!

The Ford Anglia on the road to nowhere is the new model introduced in 1959, which superseded a previous model of the same name. It was distinctive in that it had a forward-sloping rear window, designed to prevent misting up. This was not really effective, and the design was dropped on subsequent cars. The Anglia was first introduced in 1949, with an 1170cc sidevalve engine, then redesigned in 1954. The model shown was powered by a 997cc ohv engine. The lorry also stuck with a full load is the Leyland Comet, shown on page 45.

The Village Pond
Painted 1994

Could there be a greater contrast to the previous picture? A bright blue sky with sunshine, thatched cottages, hills behind, a welcoming tea shop and a pond full of tadpoles, so it must be June! The registration number FX is from Dorset, and that fits the scenery very well. It is the perfect day and place for an idyllic outing, and Dad, Mum, Grandad and the two children are making the most of it. Add to it all the cup of tea – scones and cream are not in evidence, so obviously restraint is being practised! – and this late 1930s' scene is complete.

All this pleasure has been made possible by the recent acquisition by Dad of the Morris 8 Series 2 saloon, now parked a little close to the pond. One hopes it is in gear with the handbrake firmly on, or the day might yet end in disaster! No wonder Dad is looking a little smug, for this saloon, first introduced in 1937, was the ideal family transport. Attractive and reliable, having been developed from the Series 1, it was surprisingly roomy inside, but as it had no boot, luggage had to be carried on a rack behind the spare wheel. The tourer owned by the author had an easily removable back seat which almost converted it into a pick-up truck with the hood down, a most useful feature.

The Morris 8 was powered by a four-cylinder sidevalve 918cc engine, rated at 22.5bhp and fitted with an SU carburettor. Drive was through a three-speed gearbox, without much syncromesh on any gear! The author remembers travelling the Winchester to Stockbridge road in his sister's Series 1, and at 40mph feeling as though it was going through the sound barrier! However, it must be stated that family saloon cars such as the Morris 8 brought motoring within the reach of millions of people, and the roads have been crowded ever since!

Historic pictures generally require reference from many photographs, as in many cases the scene to be portrayed no longer exists. Although this painting shows an idyllic scene many years ago it is one of pure fiction with random cottages added in such a way as to form an 'enclosed' scene and to give the impression of a safe and homely place.

Moving the Fair On
Painted 1996

Malcolm has painted a portrait here of the last Showman's engine to be used to pull a 'train' of fairground wagons, and the date for this scene is the mid 1950s. The sight of the three tarpaulin-covered wagons is a reminder of the huge and complicated organisation required to constantly unpack and pack up the travelling funfair, a task undertaken by a surprisingly small number of team members. The same organisation would apply just as much to the great travelling circuses of the day, with large and potentially dangerous animals adding an interesting extra dimension! It was the arrival of the traction engine, with its towing capacity and electrical generating ability, which made all this possible in the first place (see page 67). Such a train of wagons would never be allowed on our roads of today, and one suspects people would not be as patient as the driver of the Morris 8 waiting for the road to clear. The Morris is the same model as that shown on the previous page. The advertisements of the period, for Wills Gold Flake, milk and Guinness, all add topical colour to the scene, but one hopes that upstairs windows have been closed against the fumes. The smoke from traction engines always had a most distinctive smell.

The Showman's road engine shown was built by Burrell in 1923, and was no. 3949. It was a double-crank compound engine with a nominal horsepower of 8, and was first owned by W. Nichols of Forestgate, London, then bought by Charles Presland, of Tilbury, Essex, who owned it at the time it is pictured here.

Fairgrounds hold a fascination for young and old alike, whether it be the bright lights of the carousel or in times past the gentle rocking of a Showman's engine generating electricity. 'Princess Mary' was one of the last engines in fairground service and could be seen occasionally in the fairground on my way home from school during the 1950s. I tried unsuccessfully to draw the engine on more than one occasion, but I hope this attempt nearly forty years later is more pleasing.

AEC Regal
Painted 1995

The arrival of the motor coach meant a whole new experience became possible for the many people in the 1930s and 40s who still could not afford to own a car, even a baby Austin! For those who lived in places such as Bradford and Huddersfield the not-so-distant Lake District suddenly became within reach, and could be explored to a considerable extent in a single day's outing. The roads might still have been pretty basic, and the local sheep grazing by the side of Wastwater in West Cumbria might still be unused to such sights, but the grandeur of the scenery mixing hills and lakes was unfailingly breathtaking. The terrain also meant that driving a coach of this size along the twisting walled roads of the Lake District, hoping that if you met oncoming traffic the road would be wide enough to pass, and at the same time keeping a sharp lookout for wandering sheep, called for much care and skill on the part of the coach drivers. Doubtless before too long there would be a stop for a welcome break for driver and passengers alike and a bit of something home-made to eat at Ambleside or Grasmere.

The coach in the picture is an AEC Regal with a body made by Duple. It would have been a 37-seater. This vehicle could be powered by either a petrol or diesel engine, as the late 1930s as the period when diesel engines were coming into favour for both coaches and lorries. The AEC diesel engine used was rated a 7.7-type. With these coaches the roof was not extended out over the bonnet, as in some cases, and the drivers' difficulties were compounded on wet days by the small size of the windscreen wiper, and consequent restricted visibility.

Watching the Hovercraft

Painted 1997

In 1877 John Thorneycroft, an engineer, conceived the idea of building a boat with a cavity under the hull in which air would be trapped, causing the boat to ride higher in the water, and encounter less resistance. Later he used bellows driven by a clockwork motor, to force air into the cavity, and thus enable the vessel to ride on a cushion of air. It was the first hovercraft, perhaps, but lack of suitable power prohibited any further development. In 1955 Christopher Cockerell produced a prototype hovercraft, but it was difficult to control, and the powers-that-be could not decide whether to classify it as a ship or an aircraft! In 1959 the design was modified, and with the introduction of the 'skirt' the problem of control was solved. From then on bigger and bigger hovercraft were built, culminating in the SRN4 built by Saunders-Roe, and capable of carrying 300 passengers and 50 vehicles. This hovercraft was 185-feet long, and had a fully laden weight of 300 tons. The skirt, which weighed in at 20 tons, cost £5 million, and was of course a vital part of the construction.

One of the onlookers is very impressed by the spectacle he is watching, not least the uncanny ability of the hovercraft to move from water to land without a moment's hesitation. His companion appears more of a traditionalist! Sadly, because of high fuel costs and other factors, the hovercraft could never really compete with fast ferries, despite their many advantages, and they have now largely given up the cross-Channel routes. They are still used a great deal for military purposes, and obviously make marvellous landing craft for both troops and vehicles, as they can deliver cargo right up on to the beach. How vulnerable they would be to hostile fire is an open question.

During the period when hovercraft operated a regular cross-Channel service they carried 250 million passengers at speeds of up to 85mph. There were only two minor accidents in that time, and no passenger was injured or killed. Truly the hovercraft has been a remarkable means of transport.

Foden Steam Wagon

Painted 1998

It was undoubtedly a gentler, slower age, when people had time to stop and have a chat, even if they should have been unloading barrels! However, in this case it looks as though they have just been spotted by the landlady of the Rose and Crown, who is about to deliver a homily on the blessedness of hard work from a convenient pulpit, the upper window of the pub. She probably noticed that there was very little noise of moving barrels, and went to see what was happening; or in this instance not happening.

The Foden steam wagon in this picture is based on no. 3510, built by Foden's in 1913, and rated at 4 tons. In contrast to the Sentinel (page 119) the Foden had much the same layout as the traction engines, with cylinders above the boiler, driving a crank linked to a large flywheel, to regulate momentum. The rear wheels were then chain driven. No. 3510 was first supplied by the makers to a company in Manchester, but at the end of its working life it found its way to the Henry Ford Museum in Detroit, USA. It was brought back to Britain in 1980, and is now preserved in this country.

The Foden steam wagon was one of a number of such vehicles, made by different companies, which enjoyed limited success, and were then quickly eclipsed by the petrol and diesel lorries when they appeared on the scene in ever greater numbers. Three factors contributed to this: first, the relatively small carrying capacity of the wagon compared to the space needed for engine, fuel and driver; second, the inconvenience of having to carry about both water and coal in fairly large quantities, and the time it took to load these supplies; third, the slow speeds achievable, compared to the increasingly powerful lorries of the day.

The cart seen in the background was the ubiquitous. One hopes that by the time the barrels are delivered safely to the cellar the landlady will have simmered down enough to hand out a free pint to each of the thirsty draymen, and not send them packing off in the tumbril like those unfortunates in Paris two centuries before, who were taken in similar mode to the guillotine!

Austin Devon
Painted 1996

As a boy it seemed the bridge parapet was always a little too high wherever one went. They must have been built to a standard dimension, and one always had to stand on tiptoe on the narrow ledge, holding on tight with both hands and straining to see which track the train was on – though in this case the signal gives a valuable clue. At first the distant train does not appear to be moving at all, then it suddenly emerges from the next bridge up the line, and rushes down with increasing speed and noise, until with a roar, a cloud of smoke and steam, the watcher, the bridge and the gleaming car are all engulfed, and the train has passed. You will realise how often this author did it!

The car is an Austin Devon four-door saloon, introduced by Austin in late 1947, and a complete contrast to the Austins which had gone before in terms of styling and engine design. Its flowing lines, lack of running boards and built-in headlamps stressed the break with the past, while the interior was roomy, though the boot was rather small. It was powered by a 1200cc ohv pushrod engine, and could attain a top speed of 65mph and give 30mpg. The engine was rated at 40bhp and drove through a four-speed gearbox, with syncromesh between the upper three ratios. Excellent access to the engine compartment was provided by a rear-hinged bonnet. The model was so successful, especially in the USA, that by 1950 it had established itself as Britain's biggest dollar-earning car of all time. It was a comfortable and solid car, pleasant to ride in, but with a tendency to roll on sharper corners! It actually weighed just under a ton, but was only 13-feet long. Having also inspired a little sister, the Austin A30 (see page 71) and the larger A70 Hereford, the Devon was superseded in September 1954 by the Austin A40/50 Cambridge.

Malcolm has set this scene on the Great Western Railway in the Reading area, in the early 1950s, and he says the locomotive is a King, but you will have to take his word for it!

Nero Burning ROM

19:29:13

```
                  SCSI Exec, HA 2, TA 0, I
           Status:        0x04  (0x01,
           HA-Status       0x00  (0x00,
           TA-Status       0x02  (0x01,
           Sense Key:      0x03  (KEY_ME
           Sense Code:     0x11
           Sense Qual:     0x05
           CDB Data:       0x28      0x
           0x00 0x00 0x00
           Sense Data:     0x70  0x00  0x
           0x00 0x00 0x00      0x00  0x

#15 SCSI -1128 File Cdrd
SCSI Exec, HA 2, TA 0, I
```

THE NEXT

"A40 WAS THE SOMERSET,
THE 2 DOOR MODEL (RARE) WAS THE DORSET
THE FIRST A40 WAS THE
"HAMPSHIRE" THEN THE
"HEREFORD

Skyways' York
Painted 2000

The Avro York, first introduced into service in 1942 for use as a military transport, was designed to use the same engines, wings and tail unit as that of the already immensely successful Avro Lancaster bomber, thus greatly reducing design and production costs. After the war the plane continued in production until 1948, and in all a total of 253 were built. Many wartime aircraft were transferred to civilian use, and the transport could be found giving invaluable service all over the world during the 1950s. The York was powered by four Rolls-Royce Merlin 24 engines, rated at 1620hp each. These provided a maximum speed of 306mph and a cruising speed of just over 200mph. The range was up to 3000 miles, depending on load. Many airlines used the York for passenger and freight transport, and it had a reputation of being a very strong and reliable aircraft.

In the background to this picture can be seen an Auster light aircraft, with its distinctive high-wing monoplane configuration, and also a Douglas DC3 Dakota. An airport official in a clearly marked Ford Escort van of mid-1950s' vintage is watching the York come in to land, and probably also keeping in touch with the control tower using his short-wave radio. The Escort van was derived from the popular Anglia car produced by Ford in 1954, and was marketed as a 5cwt van, powered by the 1172cc sidevalve engine.

The aircraft portrayed, G-AGOB was built in 1946 and handed over in June of that year. It was purchased by Skyways of London, a relatively small airline, in March 1955, and was eventually withdrawn from service at Stansted in August 1962.

19:29:13

Status: 0x04 (0x01,
HA-Status   0x00 (0x00,
TA-Status   0x02 (0x01,
Sense Key: 0x03 (KEY_ME
Sense Code: 0x11
Sense Qual: 0x05
CDB Data: 0x28 0x05
0x00 0x00 0x00 0x
Sense Data: 0x70 0x00 0x
0x00 0x00 0x00 0x

#16 TRANSFER -25 File Re
Error reading data

19:29:13

#17 Text 0 File ThreadedT
all writers idle, stoppir

THE DE LUXE MODEL
WITH PSEUDO WOOD SIDE TRIM
WAS THE 'SQUIRE'

The Ford and the Vauxhall

Painted 1997

This picture takes us back to the earliest days of motoring, when many roads consisted of more mud than tarmac, and a whole range of driving clothes was an essential part of motoring. The driver did not have to bother about other traffic very much, but negotiating fords and avoiding the worst bumps and ruts required different sorts of skill. It was also the period when a passing car was such a rarity that bystanders like this little girl would stop their flower-gathering to watch it go by, and should it stop, or, better still, break down, a crowd of spectators would gather with amazing speed.

The Vauxhall shown is a 12/14 model of 1904. This was, for its day, a handsome four- to five-seat tourer, but it did not provide its passengers with either a hood or windscreen, so it is fortunate that the day is sunny. Night-driving by the light of the single paraffin-lit headlight would have been a considerable adventure, especially as a sudden gust of wind would blow out the flame without warning. Like many other cars, the Vauxhall had several vital pieces of equipment protruding at the front, such as the radiator, springs, starting handle and headlight, so a collision could be much more than just a bent bumper.

The Vauxhall company began life making engines for river craft on the Thames in the mid 1850s, and was based at Wandsworth. The name was derived from the nearby Vauxhall Pleasure Garden so famous in Regency days. The company produced its first motor car in 1903, and in November 1904 a 2.4-litre model was marketed, which had three separate vertical cylinders and cost £375. In early 1905 the Vauxhall company moved to the site in Luton which they still occupy in 2002, even though car production there has sadly ceased. The Vauxhall company had been taken over by General Motors of the USA in 1925.

Faced with cars which had no hood or windscreen yet were capable of 40mph the clothing manufacturers came into their own. Motoring clothes had to be waterproof, dustproof, windproof and fashionable! With different garments for summer and winter, a lady's motoring wardrobe could cost as much as £300 – as much as the car! Even the dog could be provided with coat, hood and goggles! In our picture the driver wears a traditional Ulster driving coat, perhaps fur lined for winter use, and a Peary cap, with folding sideflaps, while his fair companion wears a double-breasted Burberry, probably also fur lined, and a motorist's hat with veil. The driver's goggles and moustache add a dashing finishing touch!

Fuel for the Locomotive
Painted 2002

Many English pubs located near railway stations, or even lines, had appropriate names, such as the Station Hotel, the Railway Arms, and in this instance the Locomotive. This picture is based on a real pub which the artist, surprisingly, knows very well. The entrance to the cellar is reached through a chain-link fence and via a trapdoor situated at street level. The delivery man for Fremlins County Ales, having opened the fence and trapdoor, faces the challenging task of transferring many gallons from his Austin lorry to the 'tender' of the Locomotive, or the cellar as it is usually known!

Austin produced its first lorry in 1913, an unusual and very advanced forward-control model. No more lorries were produced until 1938, when the K-series of vehicles from 30cwt to 3 tons appeared. The appearance, with rounded radiator, was so similar to the Bedfords of the day that they were nicknamed 'Birmingham Bedfords'! Many saw service during the Second World War. The vehicle pictured is a K2 truck, rated as 2–3 tons, and powered by a 26.8hp six-cylinder petrol engine. An alternative Perkins' diesel engine was offered on later models. Production of this type continued until 1954. A Morris saloon from the late 1930s is hiding behind the lorry in the background.

The Fremlin family bought the brewery at Earl Street, Maidstone, Kent in 1860, when it had already been in existence for seventy years in that greatest of hop-growing and beer-brewing counties. Fremlins County Ales, with their distinctive trademark of the elephant, were brewed at a number of locations, but the company was eventually bought out by Whitbread in 1967. The brewery in Earl Street was closed in 1972, but the brand name was retained until 1997 when it was dropped by Whitbread. Luckily, the name lives on in Malcolm's evocative and thirst-quenching picture!

Royal Yacht *Britannia*
Painted 1997

The tradition of the Royal Yacht goes back to the time of Charles II, who knew all about the sea and ships, and had to leave his kingdom, and later regain it, by ship. The Royal Yacht could be both the means of royal travel, or royal relaxation. William IV, nicknamed 'The Sailor King' loved the sea and was afloat whenever possible. His niece, Victoria, however, was far from keen, but despite this had a Royal Yacht, the *Victoria and Albert* specially built, and she was to be used on many ceremonial occasions such as Spithead Reviews of the Royal Navy. George V loved sailing, and revelled in hair-raising races on his J-class yacht *Britannia*. This beautiful yacht was scuttled on the orders of his son Edward VIII.

In the early 1950s it was decided, perhaps as a gesture of defiance in a world of continuing post-war austerity, to build a new Royal Yacht, also to be called *Britannia*. To justify her cost to the taxpayer she was designed so that she could be rapidly converted into a hospital ship if need arose. Built by John Brown & Co. Ltd on the Clyde, she was launched by the Queen on 16 April 1953. She was of 5769 tons displacement, 412-feet long and with a beam of 55 feet. She had twin screws driven by two geared turbines, and was capable of 21 knots. There were special features of her design. The royal apartments were situated between the main and mizzen masts, where the motion of the ship would be least, and vibration at a minimum, and she gained a fine reputation for her excellent performance. The funnel was specially shaped to lift gases and smoke away from the deck.

She was fitted with three masts for flying the necessary three flags: the Royal Standard, the Lord High Admiral's ensign, and the Union Jack. The White Ensign was flown at the stern.

Britannia quickly gained a reputation as the world's finest ceremonial vessel. She carried a complement of 255 crew, with 21 officers and 234 other ranks. Sailors sported a distinctive black silk bow, and always wore plimsolls aboard ship to prevent undue noise disturbing the passengers. Much appreciated by all the Royal Family, she had a splendid record of service until eventually rising costs and her age forced the decision to decommission her in 1997. Perhaps money that could have been spent on her was needed for the Millennium Dome! She has now found a permanent home as a floating museum in Leith, the port for Edinburgh.

Malcolm's picture shows *Britannia* leaving John Brown's yard on the Clyde at the start of her life of service. It was specially painted for a friend who had been much involved in her design and building.

Last Day of Term
Painted 1998

The holly wreath on the cottage door proclaims that the excitement of Christmas is not far off, but there is also all the fun of a substantial snowfall. Even in the road where vehicles have passed it is still crisp and soft underfoot, and there has been enough to build a large and very smart snowman, in the traditional manner, in the cottage garden. The downside is that the school bus has managed to get through to the village, so even though it is the last day of term before the Christmas holidays, the snowman must be abandoned and school satchels gathered up to be shouldered for the last time this term. The happier thought is that as it is the last day there will probably be no proper lessons, but a host of pre-Christmas activities such as plays, parties and carol services which can be much more eagerly anticipated than maths and geography!

The sturdy school bus that the children hoped might not arrive is a Bristol L5G, a model first produced in 1946 and then updated in 1950. The bus shown, with the Essex registration number ONO 49, is one of a batch with bodies built by Eastern Coach Works and delivered to Eastern National in 1950. The model was front-engined with a back-loading saloon, but the design was changed to give a front entrance in 1952. Unlike the AEC Regal (page 99), the roof was extended to cover the bonnet on this model. The driver again had an isolated cab, keeping him cut off from whatever goings-on occurred in the saloon behind him, something many of today's drivers might envy from time to time!

The Bristol buses were produced by the Bristol Commercial Vehicle Company. Although also based in Bristol, this was a completely separate company from the Bristol Aeroplane Company which also produced Bristol cars after the Second World War. The bus manufacturing company later amalgamated with Tillings.

Leyland, the Lorry and the Clock

Painted 1997

The weather is still snowy, but the beer has to get through, and what better means than this eight-wheel Leyland Octopus, with plenty of weight over the rear axles, and enough cargo to keep the thirsty going until a thaw sets in! The Leyland Octopus was first so named in the 1930s, when a 15-ton forward-control eight-wheel lorry was produced. Further models were developed, and the one in our picture is an eight-wheel tanker from the late 1950s, used to transport a variety of bulk liquids. This one was owned by Vaux Breweries of Sunderland.

Leyland Motors began life in 1896, building steam wagons, and produced their first petrol-powered lorry in 1904. The company developed steadily, producing lorries and tanks during the world wars, and thanks to the designs of brilliant engineers such as Sir Henry Spurrier, their vehicles were always at the forefront of engineering technology. Leyland also developed the habit of buying up competitors, and over the years Albion, AEC, Scammell, Austin, Morris & Guy all came under its umbrella, among others. Today it continues to produce a range of popular lorries and vans for every purpose, as well as a range of buses and coaches.

In 1930 the general sales manager of Leyland Motors suggested an imaginative way of advertising the firm by locating clocks on all the main trunk roads, which would carry the slogan 'Leyland Motors for all Time'. Many problems, especially with the clock mechanism and bad weather, were encountered, and in the end only seven were produced. Local people were paid to wind them, and the mechanism was contained within the enclosed tower. A weatherproof tube carried the driveshaft from tower to clock, as seen in the painting of the famous clock located on the A6 1½ miles south of the summit at Shap. This clock was removed in 1970, and is now preserved, as are five of the others, one of them in Australia; one that was sent to South Africa has disappeared.

It was quite a surprise to find that this project involved an internet survey of the nation's brewers! Wm Younger was founded at Leith in 1770, moving from there eight years later. It continued to expand, and in 1931 merged with McEwans to form Scottish Breweries. Wm Younger is now part of the Scottish & Newcastle group. The Corgi model which inspired this picture was reissued in May 1996, and now costs £28, equivalent to about 14 pints of its original's contents!

Morris's Sentinel

Painted 2001

There has been a heavy shower quite recently in the night, but now at dawn the clouds are clearing, and the rays from the rising sun herald a beautiful day. Few people are stirring yet, but the Morris's lorry has a long day ahead making deliveries, so an early start is imperative. The load on lorry and trailer appears to be about 65 drums of lubricating oil, meaning much energetic work to be done. The driver could not just climb into his cab and turn a key, or even swing a starting handle. It must have taken some time to get a full head of steam up so that he could tackle the hills along the route with a fully laden trailer as well.

Sentinel steam wagons were first produced in Glasgow in 1906, but the firm then moved to Shrewsbury in 1915. Steam vehicles were efficient, reliable and virtually silent, and today would be classed as environmentally friendly. They could be found in all spheres of road haulage, but sadly, crippling taxes and legislation put an end to this form of transport. Sentinel was among the leaders, and in the 1930s its vehicles offered electric speedometer drive, automatic cylinder lubrication, self-stoking boilers, power take-off for a dynamo, tyre pump compressor and tipping gear, and load steam heaters to keep you warm! The vehicle shown, which is a DG 4-6-7-ton flat platform wagon, was made in 1931. It has a vertical boiler beneath the cab, with a working pressure of 275psi, and the chimney passes up beside the driver and out through the cab roof. The cylinders, Duplex 6 x 8in, are horizontal and placed beneath the load platform at the front, and drive is by chains to the rear wheels. The chain drive was later replaced with a conventional prop shaft.

This vehicle was first owned by Samuel Banner of Liverpool and carries the city's registration. It then passed to Paul Bros Ltd, Homepride flour mills, Birkenhead. It was sold for preservation after a long working life in 1949, passing to its present owners in 1977, who then restored it in the livery of Morris of Shrewsbury as seen in this picture. The old road sign and telegraph poles add evocative detail to this fine picture.

Fire Engine
Painted 1994

Watched by an interested audience of one, the local Dodge pump ladder sets off on an emergency call. Such vehicles played a vital role in the life of the local community, for a number of reasons. They were indeed local, on the spot when needed, so had a minimum response time. The crew, a maximum of six, knew their locality in great detail; the engine was relatively small and easily manoeuvrable in confined areas, and the crew, being local men, were in a better position to offer care and comfort to those in need of help. The crew were retained men, and would be summoned by means of the siren which can be seen mounted on the pole beside the fire station. Later on the crew were issued with personal pagers, and when more people had cars this meant they could respond quickly from further afield. It looks as though at least one of the crew has arrived in his Morris 8 Series E (see page 31). Our scene is set in the late 1950s, when the bell on the fire engine has not yet been replaced with the siren, and the vehicle shown is a Dodge that was first supplied to the Fire Service in 1958, and which lasted in service until 1971.

This fire engine carried a 400-gallon internal water tank, but as its powerful pump could move the water at a rate of 500 gallons a minute, the crew would need a source of water for any prolonged action. A fire hydrant was the easiest, but if they were out fighting a stack fire at a farm, water could be drawn from the farm pond, or a nearby stream. The ladder is a wooden model which extended to 35-feet long, and the vehicle carries a discreet blue flashing warning light. Bell and light were designed not to cause immediate panic to all motorists in the proximity, such as happens with today's machines! A number of crew members were trained to drive the appliance in case of the regular driver's absence.

The registration number of the vehicle is an Essex one, and the coat of arms on the door is that of Essex County Council, but the little Morris has migrated down from Lincolnshire in an already impressive twenty-year working life. They don't make them like they used to!

Fire engines hold the same fascination for young boys as railway locomotives. I remember this vehicle on many occasions extinguishing fires next to the track started by trains on our local railway. The bicycle shown here was my own, complete with dynamo, which always seemed to offer a great deal of resistance compared to the light produced. Another item of bicycle equipment I treasured was a battery-operated silver Pifco horn shaped not unlike a space ship.

Comb's Coach

Painted 2000

It is a showery morning, and coach no. 4 owned by Comb's coaches is returning to the garage probably having been on school duty in and around the Suffolk town of Stowmarket. The coach is dripping with water, and it is fortunate that the heavy lorry going the other way up the street towards Stowmarket parish church has a good tarpaulin sheeted down to protect its load. Meanwhile, the Duke's Head in the background serves Cobbold Ales, a Suffolk speciality and another one on our list of breweries Malcolm has known! Many towns in the 1950s and 60s had their own coach and bus companies, which not only did school duties but catered for day outings organised by the many clubs and societies in the town. Operators had to keep their costs competitive; rivals from neighbouring towns would be only too eager to muscle in on their business, and they had also to be aware that many a club secretary operated on a limited budget catering for members with only their pensions to live on. People would save up for many weeks to fund a day's trip to some stately home or the seaside. The board outside the office is probably advertising an outing arranged by the coach company itself.

The coach in this picture is a Leyland PS1, powered by the Leyland Tiger engine, and in this instance with a body built by Burlingham of Blackpool. This coach was a 33-seater, and was acquired by Combs of Battisford having started life working in St Albans, though it has a Shropshire registration number. It has been interesting to record how often buses and coaches, and trams and trolleybuses were passed on from one operator to another, presumably as the better-off updated their fleets and the poorer ones took the scraps from the rich man's table – in the shape of rather worn-out old buses! In the days before stringent safety checks some of the old vehicles were run into the ground, and were probably none too safe during their latter days.

Parked in Mr Comb's forecourt is the latest model of the Standard Vanguard, with the radiator that was restyled in 1952. The car cost £555 new, probably a good deal more than the second-hand coach had done, and was powered by a 2-litre engine which could be either petrol or diesel (the same engines were fitted to the Ferguson TE20 tractor, see page 61) and which was rated at 68bhp (petrol) and 40bhp (diesel). A top speed of 80mph was claimed for the car, and a fuel consumption of 24mpg – though it had a reputation for being even more thirsty than that. The car is a local, having an Ipswich number.

Atlantic Rendezvous
Painted 1997

This splendid picture evokes all the majesty and power of these two greatest of all the Cunarders. The *Queen Mary* was built on the Clyde by John Brown & Co. Ltd, and though laid down in 1930 was not launched until September 1934, leaving for her maiden voyage to New York in May 1936. Her building took a long time due to finance problems, and she was eventually built with a large government grant on condition that she could be used as a troopship if necessary. She was to be the first of two ships, which because of their size and speed could operate a weekly transatlantic service, where three ships had been required before. Her tonnage was 80 744, length 1019 feet and beam 118 feet. Geared Parsons' turbines drove quadruple screws and gave her a top speed of 32 knots, fast enough to take back the Blue Riband of the Atlantic and hold it until the arrival of the *United States* sixteen years later in 1952. The *Queen Mary* carried 2140 passengers and 1100 crew. On 3 September 1939 war was declared, and the *Queen Mary* sailed for New York, then to Australia to be converted as a troopship. She made 86 Atlantic crossings in this role, carrying up to 15 000 troops – a whole division. In all she carried 16 683 persons on one voyage, with her crew included.

In September 1938 the *Queen Elizabeth* was launched, and finished fitting out in February 1940. She was 83 763 tons gross, 1029-feet long and 118-feet beam, so a little larger than her sister ship, and the largest passenger ship in the world. Her maiden voyage was a famous dash to New York, evading U-boats, and then on to Australia to become a troopship like the *Queen Mary*. Churchill said the service performed by the two *Queens* shortened the war by a year.

After the war was over, both liners were reconverted to their civilian duties and set about the task for which they had been designed. For the next twenty years they operated a remarkable transatlantic service, with a huge clientele of faithful devotees. Our picture shows them meeting in mid-Atlantic some time in the 1950s, for the *Queen Mary* is now fitted with radar. In the mid 1960s their operation became unprofitable, due to competition from larger faster jet aircraft, and the decision was made to retire them.

The end was a sad one. The *Queen Mary* was unbelievably sold to Long Beach, California, for £1.2 million as a floating entertainment centre, where she remains. Why she could not have remained in the UK as a maritime museum and tribute to the UK shipbuilding industry is very strange. Sadder still was the tale of the *Queen Elizabeth*, sold first to Port Everglades, Florida, she was then passed on to a Chinese ship owner to become a floating university. While being converted she caught fire in Hong Kong harbour in suspicious circumstances, and now lies rotting there, a total wreck.

Our picture remains a reminder of two of the greatest ships the world has ever known.

Building Bricks
Painted 1998

This picture is all about strength, power and engineering ingenuity. On the winding road between Colchester and Halstead in Essex is located the Chappel Viaduct, carrying the railway line from Marks Tey to Cambridge across the valley of the River Stour on 32 magnificent brick arches. The foundation stone set in the brickwork records that it was laid on 14 September 1847, that engineer Peter Bruff designed it, and George Wythes was the contractor who built it. They must have both done their work well, using seven million bricks in the process, for it stands firm and as efficient as ever today. In those days it was the Stour Valley Railway, but in 1923 it became part of the LNER, and then British Railways in 1947.

Passing the road-sign warning of the crossroads is a Foden FG5/15 eight-wheeled flat truck taking ever more bricks either to a builders' merchant or direct to the building site. This model was produced just after the war, and features the new radiator grille and redesigned cab of that period. Foden's has already featured in this book, (pages 29 and 103) with an account of its beginnings with steam wagons. By the 1930s the company had a deserved reputation for building strong, reliable and powerful lorries, capable of hauling heavy loads like the bricks in our picture without complaining. Since the war it has gone from strength to strength, building an ever more sophisticated range of vehicles for all purposes, but still maintaining their quality and reliability.

The fun begins when this lorry, owned by the Cement Marketing Company, and registered in London, arrives at its destination. The bricks will not be on pallets of any size, and the lorry carries no hydraulic crane or forklift truck as do modern vehicles. Hopefully for the crew in the cab it will not have to all be done by hand!

The livery of the Blue Circle Company has always in my opinion been attractive, and one well worthy of representation in a painting. The Foden with its load of construction material – be it cement or bricks – forms an appropriate link with the vast construction that it has just passed under. Verticals in paintings lend themselves well to reflections, although in this case the sunlight has reduced the effect somewhat.

Docklands and the Dome
Painted 1999

The redevelopment of the Docklands area of East London has been a remarkable achievement in recent times, with Canary Wharf and St Katharine Docks outstanding. To serve this new development two new railway lines have been built. A new underground, the Jubilee Line, runs from Canning Town to Epping in one direction, and to Waterloo and Stanmore in the other. But it is the Docklands Light Railway which is both imaginative and a fascinating engineering achievement. Developed over the last ten years, two branches run from Bank and Stratford, meeting at Poplar, and then diverging to go to Becton and Lewisham via Greenwich. The line has been built in stages, and the route altered in places. For example, it passed over the old Milwall Viaduct, built originally for the London and Blackwall Railway in 1872, but long disused, but the DLR route has now been altered and the viaduct, a listed structure, is once again disused.

Much of the DLR route is raised, giving a wonderful view of surrounding London, but involving some fairly energetic climbing to get up to the stations. The trains are clean and quiet, but their main feature is that they are driverless. Not since the special Royal Mail underground line was put in to connect the Central Postal Sorting Office to the railway stations has there been such a railway, and it comes as rather a surprise the first time one boards the front carriage of the two-carriage unit, but it gives the front-seat passengers a wonderful view.

In the painting we can also see Bow Creek to the left of the railway, which indicates that this is the stretch of railway between East India Dock and Canning Town, and close to Virginia Quay from which pilgrims left for America in the sixteenth century. Behind that is the Millennium Dome, possibly the largest white elephant in the world, and the most expensive! What a difference it would have made if the *Queen Mary* had been refurbished and tied up there instead. The author looked in vain for gardens, countryside, ships and boats, classical music and wildlife in this tribute to the British way of life, and came to the conclusion that it was a tawdry and banal collection assembled by a committee of nonentities. But the building was certainly impressive, and in this picture you cannot see the contents, mercifully!

Trying to find a location where both the Dome and the Docklands Light Railway can be seen juxtaposed in a pleasant environment proved to be a difficult task. Having studied the A–Z and travelled to East London within the environs of the Dome, I realised the problem. There were too many buildings obscuring any possible picture. Bow Creek came to my rescue but only after supermarket trolleys and half a factory were eliminated under that wonderful phrase 'artistic licence'.

NO CONDUCTOR RAILS!
LONDON UNDERGROUNS
USE TWO CONDUCTOR
RAILS

```
SCSI_ERR)
OK)
SCSI_TASTATUS_CHKCOND)
DIUM_ERROR)


00 0x01 0xF4 0x00 0x00 0x00 0x20

03 0x00 0x00 0x00 0x00 0x0A
00 0x00 0x11 0x05

der.cpp, Line 371


ransfer.cpp, Line 229
g conversion
```

The Trams of Blackpool

Painted 1997

In this final picture we end as we began, with trams, and a scene set in 1946. Blackpool and trams have always gone together, and this picture vividly recalls the heyday of the tram as it cruises along the seafront with the famous Tower in the background. The trams ran on a track of standard 4 ft 8½in gauge, the same as the railways, and the two in the picture are both English Electric 1st Series railcoaches, introduced in 1933–34, and in use on the Fleetwood service. The bodies were mounted on 4ft-wheelbase trucks, and powered by two English Electric 327 motors, developing 57hp each. The open-top double-decker version behind the single-decker had seats for 56 people, and a fine view from the top deck. It was a Streamline Open Topper, and was mounted on trucks with a wheelbase of 4ft 9in. These trams were introduced in 1933–34, and used on Fleetwood service. Walter Luff was the transport manager of Blackpool Corporation when the new fleet of luxury trams was introduced into service, and he received the credit, although their purchase had been planned some time before he obtained the position. Passengers waiting for a tram would let the old ones go by so that they could ride on one of the new ones, and gentlemen would even raise their hats when entering the car in acknowledgement of the beautiful interior!

The front tram is passing a Humber Snipe 27hp of 1936 vintage, one of the Rootes Group range of cars, and beyond can be see a Tate & Lyle Leyland undertype steam wagon of 1926 design, with an enclosed Duplex engine having 4½ x 6in cylinders and roller bearings throughout. The boiler worked to 250psi and after twenty years it is still giving good, if rather smoky, service to its owners! (See page 117.)

Trams were part of everyday life in the period between the wars, and there was a famous *Punch* cartoon which showed an old lady alighting from a tram, and addressing the conductor, 'Young man, will I receive an electric shock if I place my foot on the tram rail?' To which the conductor replies, 'No ma'am, you're quite safe unless you put the other foot on the overhead wire!'

It is interesting to note that in this picture there appears to have been a central rail at some time (see page 15), but this is now no longer in use.

Bibliography

ALLEN M. *British Saloon Cars of the Fifties,* Haynes Publishing Group (1995)

ALLEN C., STONE J., MACMILLAN N. *Railways, Ships and Aeroplanes,* Odhams Press, London (1946)

BRAZENDALE K., ACETI E. *Classic Cars, The World's Finest Designs,* Macdonald, London (1988)

CASTLE C. *Clydebank 100 ships from Clydebank and District,* West Dunbartonshire Libraries & Museum (1996)

COLEMAN T. *The Liners,* Penguin Books, Norwich (1977)

DELAHOY R. *Southend Corporation Transport Trams, Trackless and Buses,* Yarnacott Publications, Southend-on-Sea (1986)

EAGLES B. *Liners of Southampton and the Solent,* Waterfront, Kingfisher Productions, North Yorkshire (1999)

FAITH N. *Classic Ships – Romance and Reality,* Boxtree, Great Britain (1995)

      Classic Trucks – Power on the Move, Boxtree, Great Britain (1995)

FLOWER R., JONES M. *One Hundred Years of Motoring, An RAC Social History of the Car,* McGraw-Hill Co-Publications, Maidenhead (1981)

GRIEVES R. *Truckin' round Scotland,* Arthur Southern Ltd, Midlothian (1997)

HAROLD A. *Camera above the Clouds, Vol. 2 – The Aviation Photographs of Charles E. Brown,* Airlife Publishing, Shrewsbury (1985)

MARRIOTT L. *Civil Aviation Review – Second year of issue,* Ian Allen, Surrey (1985)

Observer's Book of Ships, Automobiles & Aircraft, Frederick Warne, London.

PRIPPS R., MORLAND A. *Ford and Fordson Tractors,* Motorbooks International, Osceola, USA (1995)

STEVENS-STRATTEN S. *British Lorries 1900–1992,* Ian Allen, Surrey (1991)

      Light Commercial Vehicles, Ian Allen, Surrey (1991)

TAYLOR M. *Lotus Elan – The Complete Story,* The Crowood Press, Wiltshire (1996)

VANDERVEEN B. *British Cars of the Late Thirties 1935–1939,* Frederick Warne, London (1979)

WARREN P., LINSKEY M. *A Photographic History Taxicabs,* Almark Publishing, Surrey (1976)

Index